Last Will

And

Testament

God's bequest to you

Deon Stevens

Revised Edition

NLT: Scripture quotations marked (NLT) are taken from the Holy Bible, New Living Translation, copyright © 1996. Used by permission of Tyndale House Publishers, Inc., Wheaton, Illinois 60189. All rights reserved.

Scripture taken from THE AMPLIFIED® BIBLE, Old Testament copyright © 1965, 1987 by Zondervan Corporation. The Amplified New Testament copyright © 1958,1987 by the Lockman Foundation. Used by permission.

Scripture taken from THE MESSAGE. Copyright © by Eugene H. Peterson, 1993,1994,1995. Used by permission of NavPress Publishing Group.

GBN: Scriptures marked as "(GBN)" are taken from the Good News Bible – Second Edition © 1992 by American Bible Society. Used by permission.

NKJV: Scriptures noted NKJV are taken from the NEW KING JAMES VERSION. Copyright © 1979, 1980, 1982, Thomas Nelson, Inc., Publishers.

JB: The Jerusalem Bible. Copyright © 1966 by Darton, Longman and Todd, LTD., and Doubleday & Company, Inc.

KJV: The King James version of the Bible.

Quotations taken by permission from Brennan Manning's, Lion and Lamb, published by Flemming H. Revell, a division of Baker Publishing Group, copyright © 1986.

This is a revised version of a book by the same name first published in 2006.

ISBN 0-620-35931-5

www.deonstevens.wordpress.com

DEDICATION

I dedicate this book to my grandparents, Ivor and Lettie Stevens, who pointed the Stevens family God-wards. They walked at a level of faith way ahead of their time. Their seven children and many grandchildren made a remarkable contribution to the church, business, community and society in general. I am eternally grateful to my cousin, Mike Loppnow for explaining the way of salvation to me.

I had the distinct privilege of growing up in a gracious environment. My parents, Frank and Lettie have a natural way of showing God's grace to their family, friends and acquaintances—their lives mirror the loving kindness and tender mercies of the God they know so intimately.

Susan, my loving wife of 46 years, continues to believe in me, and has the grace to accept me just as I am—always the same, she has a natural way of adding happiness to any gathering—adding something really special to family, friends and most especially to me. Thank you for encouraging me to complete the book. You are the best part of my life. I love you dearly!

I am especially blessed to be the father of three lovely daughters, Carmen, Michele and Jacqueline, who continue in my grandfather's pattern of living, carrying faith to the next generation. I love you dearly!

ACKNOWLEDGEMENTS

Had it not been for that dreary afternoon while sitting idly on the sofa, bored stiff, surfing TV channels, I would not have accidentally come across a nameless preacher who forever changed the way I relate to God the Father. He showed me that my personal Christian performance had no influence upon God's love towards me. I later came to discover that his name was John Sheasby. His teachings have given me an insightful perspective into God's character, and brought new clarity to my fuzzy understanding of His gracious nature. At last I had found the keys to the treasure chest of my inheritance. The first key was to accept that I am entirely in right-standing with God, and the second was to accept that I am loved in my present less than perfect condition. God is exceedingly generous, unconditionally merciful, unreservedly kind, and wholeheartedly in love with each and every one of us.

The bottom line was, that my best efforts to win God's favour, had gotten me nowhere. I had made and broken far too many promises. Was I alone, or was this also the experience of my church compatriots?

Judging by their smiling faces, they seemed to be getting it right. But then again, if they were judging me by the perfect image I was attempting to portray, they probably thought I was getting it right. Was our Christianity really that shallow? Could it be that they were every bit as disillusioned with religion as I was!

I have subsequently discovered that God's favour is not for sale—it cannot be bought with good deeds, not even with exemplary behaviour. That kind of thinking had gotten me nowhere.

God's favour simply cannot be earned. Grace means undeserved favour, and we do well to leave it at that. I have subsequently come to realise that blessings are not granted for something we have or have not done; they're granted for what Jesus did! There is simply no need for frenetic buzzing about in the hope of being noticed for our piety. Try as we may—there is nothing a mortal can do to impress the supreme creator of the universe!

I was convinced that religion held all the answers—convinced that a relationship with God was only possible by diligently adhering to religion's many rules. But I had to admit that, a lifetime of striving for His favour, had been pretty fruitless. Frankly, looking back, religion had failed to deliver on its many promises!

As with a box of jumbled jigsaw puzzle pieces, the complexity of Christian doctrines can be pretty daunting. How do all the pieces fit together? But when I began to view the very same Bible concepts through the prism of His "undeserved love" for me, the fog lifted, and the gospel took on new meaning. I had to admit that, as much as I had thought I knew the Bible, I had missed the essence of the gospel. My skewed knowledge of God's grace had distorted my perception of His goodness.

It took a revelation of my heavenly Father's passionate love for me to adjust my perspectives. His passion set my passion ablaze! I soon discovered that nothing comes close to the sublimity of a divine romance! My utmost strivings to earn His favour had failed, leaving me with feelings of guilt and unworthiness—enough to block my faith, thus stemming the flow of His favour to me.

People like Francis Frangipane, Max Lucado, Brennan Manning, Bob Mumford, Steve Mc Vey and Andrew Womack, helped fill in the gaps with their liberating understanding of God's unfailing love.

Jerry Savelle and Charles Capps helped me to see the faith connection to grace. God has blessed His people with so many enlightened teachers, each bringing another aspect to complete the picture of a generous loving Father, who is more willing to give than we are to receive!

CONTENTS

I believe that Deon is a strategic champion of a Glorious Grace revolution taking place throughout the earth. Thank you so much Deon for your courage and compassion. I honor you and salute you in His abundant Grace.

Rob Rufus, Pastor of City Church International Hong Kong.

PREFACE

Do you believe that followers of Jesus should be better off on this planet than non-followers? Do you believe that Jesus made a way for us to have health, prosperity, love, joy, peace, patience, kindness, goodness, faithfulness, gentleness, and self-control? Have you ever asked yourself why this is not a reality in your life? Maybe being honest would be too much like admitting religious defeat. But, as difficult as it may be to admit, you know that what you are experiencing is somewhat less than He promised in His word.

Have you ever wondered what happened to the enthusiasm you once had as a new believer? Maybe, like me, you felt somewhat unworthy of God's favour?

Ever wondered if your church compatriots are asking themselves the same questions? Ever felt reluctant to risk bringing unbelievers to church? Would they really be impressed with religiousness?

Ever wondered why so many ministers of the gospel fall into the very same sins they so passionately preach against?

There are so many more questions that we may not be brave enough to ask. There seems to be a missing link somewhere. I believe that the missing link is in our understanding of the character of God. Have we come to believe Him to be disappointed and angry with us?

A clearer understanding of His nature and of our identity in Him is needed. It's not about pleading for favours. Faith is audacious—boldly claiming inheritances bequeathed to us!

In my experience, we know that God can do anything, but we're not always equally confident of His willingness to answer our prayers. Sadly, God's many promises to favour us are often relegated to the realm of improbability.

Although we will never fully comprehend the enormity of His love for us, the exploration of it is immensely exhilarating and gloriously edifying! In discovering how desirable we are to Him, we get a shot in the arm of self-value serum! It never ceases to amaze me—His love has a way of bringing out the very best from the very worst of us! Besides, the better we understand His love, the more embolden we become to step out and expect the best from Him.

His love opens the way for us to find meaning, purpose and direction for our lives. We are blessed with glorious favour—more than we could ever wish for! How do we explain—although, the Supreme Emperor of the entire universe, yet He is not aloof and disinterested!

Why would He want to associate with the likes of you and me? From His choice of friends, it is obvious that He does not pick the comeliest of companions. Truth be told, He fell in love with us before we made any attempt to make ourselves acceptable to Him. He has invited us to be intimate with Him in His palatial throne room of grace—a place where His favour is generously dispensed!

Forget everything that you have heard about Jesus if it doesn't begin and end with love

MY DILEMMA

I am certainly not a theologian—not by any stretch of the imagination. I am still trying to get my head around the unqualified generosity and goodness of God towards each and every person on the face of the Planet. How do we explain it? Let's be reasonable: Who would continue loving the very people that scorn them. Be honest, would you love people who purposely ignore you? How about those who despise you?

Well, God has chosen to love people who openly spurn His gracious generosity. Their contempt, and at times, outright hatred of Him, does not for a moment change the way He feels about them. I just don't get it! To my untheological mind, such reckless love borders on insanity! Way beyond rationality!

How do I explain why He would give a sinner like me a brand-new spirit, perfect in every way, for no reason other than that I called on His name? Although worthy of despise-ment, He chose to love me all the same. Why would He be so forgiving? Is there no end to His tolerance?

My sincerest commitments to Him seem so piffling—so empty! After so many broken promises, why would He even bother with me, let alone woo me with loving enticements? He could just as easily ignore me for my self-seeking narcissism. Is there no end to His love? Surely, if he really knew me, He would not want anyone to know that He associates with me. Yet He allows me to use His name publicly.

The sheer joy of a clean slate and a fresh restart in life was my greatest windfall! But reality soon kicked in—as much as I tried, I was not doing a good job of keeping my slate all that clean. It soon became apparent that I had not stopped sinning. Try as I may, I simply could not shake iniquities that couldn't possibly be pleasing to Him.

The way I understand it, a partnership has no purpose unless both parties to it benefit from the relationship. But for the life of me, I could not see what God was getting out of this one. What could He possibly be getting out of my fickle end of the deal? It would seem that I am the sole beneficiary!

This kind of lopsided arrangement is not supposed to work. He gives and I receive. Could God have chased me down for the sole purpose of lavishing favour upon me? Surely any reasonable person would expect reciprocation! Yes, I surrender my life to Him and love Him, but what is the value of feeble reciprocations tinged with self-interest? As much as I wish I could claim to be selfless, I know myself better than that. And besides, what kind of a deal was it for God—He went so far as to put the curse of my sin upon His beloved Son to prevent it falling upon me!

What could I possibly give in return? Unreliable commitments, shabby deeds and one self-centred life? Is that the best I can offer? Even though I didn't set out to be unreliable, shabby and self-centred, I am plain and simply incapable of any better.

They say that there are no free lunches. In business, you get nothing for nothing. But what I discovered of Jesus is different. I am completely loved and accepted just as I am. The thought of it is intoxicating—almost too good to be true! But, if perchance there is any truth to it, can you imagine the possibilities?

After my conversion, with so much going for me, I desperately wanted to change my lifestyle, but found the task to be beyond me. Even after many years, my behaviour, though in the process of change, is still far from perfect. As disappointing as this is, I suppose I am not too different to most ordinary folk on the path called sanctification.

Let's face it, the quest for flawlessness is endless! An entire lifetime is not long enough to attain perfection. Even if we were granted a hundred lifetimes, try as we may, we would still fall horribly short of God's perfect standard. It didn't take me too long to discover that my sincerest strivings had been fruitless!

I tried to keep the Ten Commandments, but soon realised that I was botching the job! I have never even managed to stick to a New Year's resolution for all that long—not for the lack of trying, I might add. Too many destructive issues in my life remained unresolved. Not that anybody else knew about them. How could I share them with religious folk? They were far too perfect to understand. As much as I wanted to change, I found myself powerless to make anything stick. In sheer desperation, I turned elsewhere for a solution.

Humanism was an obvious choice. Maybe I could do it by positive thinking, self-affirmation, goal setting and self-discipline. At last I thought I had found the way to modify my behaviour. I was impressed with myself. Then one day, when I found myself cornered, I discovered that my old ways were still lurking in the background, ready to pounce when least expected. Alas! My flawed attitudes betrayed my best intentions!

Why was this? It later became apparent that it was not my actions that needed modification; it was my heart! My actions were merely a reflexion of deeper issues. No matter how determined I was to change, my old hang-ups kept haunting me. My modified behaviour was delicately thin—superficial at best! I needed to know how to change what was driving my actions and reactions—something had to change at a deeper level.

In my search, I turned to my church, hoping they would have the answers. I trusted the church. Afterall, this was where I had received the best gift ever given to any person—eternal life! This time I was sure I had come to the right place. My church offered me a way out in the form of rules and instructions. The problem was, no matter how hard I tried, I found myself powerless to keep them. Instead of the church providing a solution, it simply added to the problem in the form of more reasons to despise myself—**leaving me with** guilt and shame—my only trophies. Alas, the church had no viable answers. Now, desperate for help—who else could I turn to?

Then after many years of devotion to my God and church, I finally grasped the essence of the gospel—it was a darn side simpler than I had imagined. It was all wrapped up in one simple concept—nothing more than the concept of "mercy and grace"!

I was told that mercy implied that I would not get what I rightly deserved, and that grace implied that I could get what I did not deserve. I knew I deserved God's wrath, but thankfully, mercy let me off the hook—I would not get the punishment I so rightly deserved. Sounded good to me! By the same token, I knew that I did not deserve God's favour, but grace made a way for me to get what I did not deserve. Sounded even better! I learnt that the acronym for G R A C E is 'God's Riches At Christ's Expense'.

All good and well, but I still had to contend with my many hang-ups. At my wits end—what were the chances that I would ever overcome them?

Then, seemingly by chance, I discovered another dimension of grace. Grace is not only undeserved favour; it is also God's empowerment to overcome my penchant for sinning. Grace, an expression of God's infinite love, had the power to change me from within!

Love and acceptance has a way of boosting one's sense of personal value. With improved self-esteem, improved actions soon followed. They came about without effort. In my awakening to the depths of His love for me, I realised that my religious paradigms were changing for the better. Without realising it, my actions had taken a turn for the better—something for which I could take no credit.

To my surprise, I discovered that I had been going about it the wrong way around. My best efforts to master my outward actions had done nought to change me inwardly. How could they? It simply doesn't work that way! It takes more than human resolve to change deep seated paradigms—we are held captive by them! It took a while for me to understand that change does not start with modified actions; it starts with modified hearts. It takes nothing less than being loved, in the way that only God loves, to modify a person's self-image. Thereafter improved self-esteem does the rest, as it works its way into our actions.

No wonder I had failed! I needed something to change on the inside. My dogged attempts at pleasing God had only served to wear me down!

To be perfectly honest, in the absence of inner change, I had been faking it. But my faking could only be taken so far. When caught off guard, my behaviour would simply revert, letting me down as usual. I had to admit that the religious stuff I was into had failed to change me inwardly. I needed more than religion—more than my best attempts to contrive good deeds and kindness.

This is where grace came in—it could do this for me. This was the bonanza of all bonanzas—a pearl of great value—the answers I so earnestly sought were wrapped up in grace! This was the second greatest discovery of my life—a dream come true! At last I had found the power to have genuine victory over the errant ways that had so doggedly plagued me. There was no further need to strive for change. My behaviour simply fell into line with the new values that God's love had instilled into my heart.

I discovered that God loves me just as I am—not even expecting any promises from me to improve. Wow! Another windfall! What a marvellous discovery! Believe me, nothing is more reassuring than God's love, especially when we realise that it is unconditional—the ultimate boost to personal value! With this kind of edification, destructive behaviour soon lost its appeal. Does this sound too good to be true? It didn't take too long for me to accept its authenticity!

As unlikely as it may seem, I am loved and cherished in my less than perfect condition! A discovery that transformed my outlook on life. His love was adjusting my inner values and desires without any assistance from me. Offensive behaviour soon gave way to something more akin to godliness. Sheer grit and determination had failed me— my imbedded paradigms were too stubborn for that! Thankfully, as I discovered ever deeper levels of God's love for me, I found myself processing everyday challenges differently.

For as long as I was of the opinion that God was unhappy with my performance, I had reason to loath myself, and this loathing spilled over into loathing others. Endless religious striving had only resulted in self-recrimination. The harder I tried to fix myself, the more I failed. My sincerest efforts had sent me into a downward tail spin of guilt and shame!

But when I came to understand that He loves me regardless of my less than perfect state, I found myself more able to love and accept myself. How liberating! At last, the pressure was off! The mere discovery of how highly I am valued by God, was reason enough to stop seeking significance in all the wrong places.

As my understanding of God's love for me increased, my need to strive for holiness decreased. I noticed that my desires for certain things had changed—not something for which I could take any credit. The way that God values me, gave me reason to value myself in a healthy way.

It was not a onetime fix, but rather a lifelong progression of Holy Spirit influence. More of His love and acceptance equated to less appetite for sin.

I am often surprised to discover that yet another embarrassing issue no longer bugs me—so effective is His love! While my values and desires were being adjusted by His love, the need for self-restraint dwindled—love was taking care of that without my help. Unhealthy behaviour was losing its appeal.

At first, there was this niggling thought at the back of my mind. We need a little sin here and there to spice life up a bit. It's only natural to think that life would be dull without a little risqué-ness. Surprisingly, less sinning did not equal less fulfilment. Just knowing that I am loved when I don't deserve it, was immensely fulfilling in and of itself! What I found so wonderful about divine honour, was that public approval mattered less to me. I seemed to respond to life's challenges differently—the need for self-promotion came to an end. With God's love, what others thought of me mattered less.

Yes, I have shortcomings, but rather than take me down, they make me all the more appreciative of His favour. It reminds me that I am not favoured for anything I have or have not done. To be honest, I cannot give a single reason as to why He would want to bless me, yet He does! The thought of being loved, whether well behaved or not, is intoxicating! My behaviour is no longer the issue; the issue is that, as fickle as my commitment is, I remain every bit as much family of the most-high God.

This is the record of my journey of discovery. I trust that you too will find out more about God's goodness, and about the good He wants to bestow upon you. Maybe you will discover that He really isn't the person you have been led to believe Him to be. Allow me to share what I have discovered about His loving nature, our true identity in Him, and a covenant of incredible blessings!

When God makes a promise, it is a vow, leaving Himself no room to change His mind or to renege on what He has promised. We can rest assured: He is totally committed to fulfil, to the enth degree, every promise He has ever made to us!

Just knowing that we are exceedingly desirable to Him, is reason enough to raise our expectations, elevate our faith, get more from life and to turn us into more of a blessing to those around us. He is not out to zap us, nor to put a damper on the joy of living; He is out to infuse our lives with richness, overflowing with super abundant life and good cheer!

LAST WILL AND TESTAMENT

I, Jesus, formerly of Nazareth now residing in Heaven do hereby revoke, cancel and annul all Wills, Codicils and/or other testamentary dispositions heretofore made by me, and declare this to be my last Will and Testament.

I hereby nominate and appoint you, my child to be a co-heir with me of my entire estate in the event of my death.

Any property not immediately withdrawn by faith will be held in trust and be available to you, the beneficiary, whenever required. I hereby appoint the Holy Spirit as the sole trustee, and instruct Him to make all disposals without restriction to beneficiaries. Beneficiaries are hereby authorised to use the name of Jesus when making withdrawals. All such withdrawals will be honoured.

The bequest includes, among others, the following:

- Co-ownership of all that I own (Rom 8:17).
- All the blessings that were promised to Abraham (Gal 3:14).
- A complete release from any obligation contained in previous Testaments (Heb 8:13).

- No obligation to fulfil the law—I have fulfilled it on behalf of beneficiaries (Gal 3:13).
- Complete freedom from the curse of the law—I have become a curse in their stead (Gal 3:13).
- Free access to the throne of grace—beneficiaries obtain unrestrained measures of mercy, grace and help in time of need (Heb 4:16).
- The Power of Attorney to use My name to obtain anything from the Father (Matt 21:22).
- Authority to bind or lose anything. Whatever they choose to bind on earth, will be bound in heaven (Matt 16:19).
- Authority to obtain whatsoever things beneficiaries "say". All declarations of faith will be honoured (Matt 11:23).
- Authority to move mountains. (Mark 11:23)
- Free access to intimate fellowship with Me and My Father (1 John 1:3).
- Every single sin committed by beneficiaries will be forgiven (1 John 1:9).
- Beneficiaries are granted eternal accommodation with the Father in Heaven (John 3:16).
- Entitled to draw life in all its abundance (John 10:10).
- Access to healing (1Pe 2:24).
- Access to material provision (Phil 4:19).
- Access to divine guidance and counsel (Isa 58:11, 30:21).
- Endowed with the peace of God, which passes all understanding (Phil 4:7).
- Endowed with the gifts of the Spirit (1 Cor 12:28).
- Fellowship with fellow believers (1Jn 1:7).
- Ever present Holy Spirit (John 16:7).

- A re-fashioning of character by the Spirit (Rom 8:13).
- Supernatural empowerment to overcome (Rom 8:37).
- Insights into My love towards them (Eph 3:14-19).
- Divinely loved in an unmerited "Agape" way (Eph 3:19).
- Access to divine favour without merit (Rom 5:5).
- Unqualified mercy (Rom 11:32).
- Everything they set their hands to will prosper (Ps 1:3).
- Granted everything necessary for godly living (Eph 1:3).
- Divine empowerment to overcome their penchant for sinning (Rom 8:26).
- Authority to appropriate any promises contained in the scriptures (2 Cor 1:20).
- Authority to overcome with the blood of the lamb and with the word of their testimony (Rev 12:11).

None of the above benefits are subject to the fulfilment of any conditions as set out in previous Testaments (i.e. Old Testament). The Executor is authorised to honour all bequest claims upon proof of entitlement. A born-again birth certificate accompanied by faith shall serve as proof.

In witness hereof, I have hereunto set my hand at the throne of the most high God on this the day before the world was created in the presence of the scribing witnesses, all being present at the same time and signing our names in the presence of one another.

Testator: *Jesus*   As Witnessed: 1. *God the Father*

2. *Holy Spirit*

Death Certificate

It is hereby attested that Jesus of Nazareth was pronounced dead on the 1 April 0033. The cause of death was a broken heart for being blamed by Me, His Father, for everybody's sins. The weight of carrying the curse of the law proved too much to bear. Contributing factors to His death were wounds for everybody's transgressions, bruises for everybody's iniquities and deep stripes upon His back for everybody's sicknesses and diseases. At His passing, the Temple veil was ripped in two, allowing free access into the Holy of Holies.

His execution served as full and final payment for everybody's sins. Clemency is granted to whomsoever asks for it. Such individuals will receive a new identity and will not be required to die for their sins. The punishment due for their sins has been fully served by My Son. The curse of the law no longer applies to such individuals. My Son has fulfilled the law on their behalf. My judgement has been fully satisfied.

Signed: *God the Father*

This day: 1 April 0033

Which Testament Applies?

"When God speaks of a new covenant, it means he has made the first one obsolete. It is now out of date and ready to be put aside" (Hebrews 8:13 NIV). *"He cancels the first covenant in order to establish the second".* (Hebrews 10:9 NLT)

God left two testaments to mankind. The first one (The Old Testament) was conditional—subject to the fulfilment of a list of requirements. The last one (The New Testament) is an outright bequest—entirely unfettered by any qualifying conditions. It is subject only to the willingness of beneficiaries to accept ownership of their inheritances. However, beneficiaries can forfeit their inheritances if: (a) they are unaware of their inheritances; (b) they fail to take ownership of what's rightfully theirs by inheritance; (c) they mistakenly believe bequests to be subject to the qualifying conditions of an earlier testament.

With such a glorious inheritance, how is it possible that so many of us live below par? The answer could be that we are simply unaware that we have been specifically named in Jesus' Will as beneficiaries to receive an equal and joint share with Him. Of course, if we are trying to make ourselves worthy of our inheritance by striving to meet the qualifying criteria of a previous testament, we will be equally disqualified. The "Last Will and Testament" specifically disallows such tactics.

What does common law have to say when more than one testament is found upon the death of a Testator? The law is clear. The latest testament supersedes all previous testaments, rendering them null and void. Any conditions contained in them, have no standing in law. Only the wishes of the Testator, as stated in the latest testament apply.

In this "Last Will and Testament", we are named by the Testator as joint-heirs together with Christ, and as such, are given free of charge, full entitlement to all jointly bequeathed assets. They belong to both Jesus and us.

What is the extent of our inheritances? It is every promise contained in the scriptures. We have not come to the genie that appeared from Aladdin's lamp when he rubbed it—we are not limited to three wishes—we have thousands upon thousands of promises, each appropriate to our every trial, temptation, hardship and dream. We are promised health, strength, riches, joy, peace, purpose etc. No dream is too small; no dream too big. God's dream for us always exceeds our capacity to dream!

Your brother died and left you a fortune. He left you two wills. You had to look at the dates to establish which one was valid. The earlier one, with its conditional inheritances was invalidated by a more recent one. The last one is an outright bequest without conditions. If you do not take delivery of your bequest, you forfeit it. If you feel unworthy of it and would like to prove your worthiness through good works, the executor is not empowered to pay rewards—his mandate is to disperse assets in accordance with the wishes of the testator—period! He requires that you either fetch your inheritance or forfeit it!

The above is a true story about you the reader. Your older brother has died. His name is Jesus. You have come into the greatest inheritance that the world has ever known. You are much richer than you could ever imagine. You do not have to clean up your act before being allowed to take ownership. The executor will hand over all property mentioned in the will, based purely upon the fact that you are unequivocally named as a beneficiary. But he cannot do this unless you present your claim.

SIMPLY GRACE

Most of my life was spent in legalistic churches which preached the grace of God mixed with a touch of Old Testament Law and a dash of denominational legalism for good measure.

Like most believers in this environment, I felt it more prudent to keep my weaknesses to myself. How could I possibly expect perfect Christians to understand an imperfect Christian like me? Better to act out what perfect Christians would expect of perfect Christians.

Sadly, my best shot at contriving perfection, only succeeded in making me weird. My Christian compatriots always seemed to be perfect. But then again, it didn't take too long to discover that they were playing the same flaky game with me. We all felt the need to do whatever it took to gain acceptance in our pious circles. We were expected to look alike, think alike, talk alike and act alike. In short, it took some serious religious pretending to convince each other that we were decent.

Unfortunately, the moment a major disagreement arose, we were suddenly confronted with what was hidden behind our "holy" facades. And what we saw in each other was not at all pretty. Suddenly close friends were confronted with the reality of what was hidden behind each other's facades. What was thought to be mutual love, turned out to be shallowness disguised in charm—fabricated religious falsehoods masquerading as grace.

Facades can be comfortable. They allow us to lead double lives. With them, we find acceptance with fellow congregants, while keeping our shortcomings hidden. For as long as our contrived behaviour meets with religious approval, the pressure is off—our embarrassing shortcomings and true feelings can remain hidden. We dare not let on that we are somewhat less than the perfect images we portray. Our religious reputations are at stake!

One day I heard grace expounded in a way that I had never heard before. Though excited at the prospect, it was nevertheless offensive to my religious paradigms, and at first, seriously confusing. It forced me to examine my holy cows. Treasured paradigms had been indelibly imprinted onto my psyche over a lifetime of diligent church going.

Slowly but surely, as I allowed the Holy Spirit to reveal ever greater truths about my Father's unwavering love for me, I came to understand how extravagant His grace really is—an enormously overwhelming discovery! How could I have lived so religiously yet have misconstrued the most crucial point of the gospel? How could years of diligent church going have revealed so much to me, yet left me in the dark concerning the basics? It's not that it was something new, it's the old, old story. His patience and loving kindness had always been in my Bible, but years of legalistic indoctrination had prevented me from coming to grips with it!

Even the Pastors of our local church, who initially bought into the concept of the goodness of God, later turned from it, reverting back to performance driven Christianity imbedded in religious tradition. This bothered me, because at the time, one of the pastors was so taken with God's grace that he destroyed his whole life's work of preaching notes and apologised to the congregation for having misled them for so many years.

His shift from a works based Christianity to a grace based Christianity was enormously convincing—leading many congregants into glorious liberation, way beyond their wildest dreams. But then, to the utter bewilderment of the congregation, he abandoned his new understanding of grace, and reverted back to a performance based Christianity.

I asked him what had brought about such a dramatic reversal to his thinking. His answer completely floored me. He said that he still held to his views on the grace of God, but that grace could not be applied to all people equally. Some would take advantage of their liberty and misuse it to justify their sin. He quoted a particular problem with a group of people who work the winelands of the Western Cape. He was convinced that they would misuse such unqualified freedom to indulge in alcoholism. Alcoholism is unfortunately the way of life of many of these farm workers.

This led me to look a little deeper into the question of the goodness of God. Here is what I discovered. *"But where sin increased, grace increased much more"* (Rom 5:20 GNB). In other words, the worse the sinner, the more grace is afforded by God to help overcome his or her sin. He does not grant less grace to more sinful individuals, He grants them more grace! In so doing, He is not granting them licence to continue sinning, but rather granting them empowerment to overcome their penchant for sinning.

Let's face it, God does not hate sinful humanity; He is in love with sinful humanity, so much so that He sent His beloved Son to the cross for the worst of the worst of us. Sin is a condition common to all mankind, whether religious or not. And grace is God's love language—not only to the pious, but also to the most despicable of humanity. Clearly, if it were not for grace, sin would be unfixable. Sin would rule out any possibility of a divine romance between God and mankind. A holy God simply cannot have a relationship tainted with sin. But thankfully, grace enables Him to overlook our sin. Seriously? Can this really be so? Does it actually stretch that far? If true, how incredibly fortunate we are!

If He can love us just as we are, then who are we to disagree with Him? His love gives us permission to love ourselves. We only look for value in sin because we have not found value in God's love. The more value we find for ourselves in His love, the less appetite we have for sin. Sin's glitter simply fades, and its allure weakens as we find ourselves inexplicably losing interest in it.

Allow me to re-emphasise this point. Sinning saints need more grace than so called "holy" saints. Worse sin simply cannot be restrained with a lesser amount of grace. This pastor was affording more grace to the ones who needed less change, and less grace to the ones who needed more change—precisely opposite to what was required.

Grace doesn't set us free to sin—it sets us free from sin! I discovered that grace does not give us permission to sin; it gives God permission to use His love to change our affections for sin. Being undeservedly loved has a profound impact on the way we live—genuine victory over sin soon follows—and nobody seems to have an explanation for it.

When He is changing us by His grace, we are not left to fruitlessly strive to change ourselves. It is not our behaviour; it's our hearts that He changes, and inevitably, Christ-like hearts produce Christ-like behaviour. When this happens, there is no further need to struggle with our weaknesses. Besides, striving is profoundly futile!

A new convert friend of mine felt pressurised by the church to stop smoking. He enjoyed smoking and was getting through about two packs a day. Finally, he agreed to pray about it. This was his prayer, "Lord I like smoking, and I am going to smoke for the rest of my life. If you don't like it, you will have to change my heart". Surely this was not correct praying. It certainly wasn't the way I was taught.

Well, the proof is in the pudding. He never smoked another cigarette. No striving, no withdrawal symptoms, just no more desire for smoking. He didn't try to modify his behaviour. In an instant he just supernaturally lost his taste for the dastard habit. Although he didn't pray to stop smoking, he did pray for a changed heart, didn't he? Obviously, his changed heart didn't enjoy smoking. In an instant, smoking supernaturally became repulsive to him.

It has taken me a while to discover what I know of God's goodness. Even if I devote the rest of my life to learning about His grace, I am convinced that I will never get to the point where I can say that I fully grasp just how wide, how long, how high, how deep His love and goodness towards us really is (Eph 3:18,19).

What is God's purpose for us? If it were just to save us from eternal damnation, then why didn't He just rapture us immediately after we were born-again? He must have had a good reason for leaving us here. He told Abraham that He would bless him so that he could be a blessing to others.

The blessing does not stop with us. Like Abraham, we are here to pass it on to others. But before we can do so, we must have something of value to pass on. We can only bless others out of what we have received from Him. God desires to channel His awesome goodness, mercy and grace through us to hurting humanity. I believe that God is saying, "I want to show you off to the world—lavish My favour upon you—show others how big my love really is".

When we allow ourselves to be loved in such an unqualified way, we find ourselves loving others in an unqualified way. From our overflow, we edify, encourage and uplift anybody who has the good fortune to bump into us. God uses us as conduits of His favour to enrich others. He has deputised us to be His agents for change to the world around us—equipping us to encourage, edify, uplift, fortify, heal, comfort, support, bring hope to the hopeless, peace to the troubled and joy to the depressed.

Of course, it goes much further than that—we are saved to take dominion, and to reign over life's challenges. As we become more aware of His presence within, we discover a power that enables us to be in command—to be the head and not the tail—to cease to be intimidated by the curve balls that come our way.

As I progressed along the journey of discovering the truths of His grace, I would occasionally come across gainsayers who would sow confusion into my new cherished understandings, and before realising what had happened, I would be drawn back into the trap of performing for God's favour.

With the very best of intensions, the flawed message of striving for God's favour is often preached from our pulpits. But it serves only to draw us away from His grace. Religious performance seems so right, so pious, yet so enormously destructive to the treasured concepts of the gospel. Let's face it—without grace, what are we left with? Religion? Is that all we have? There is no question about it; without grace of the most extreme kind, we have absolutely nothing at all!

Are good works not good then? Of course they are good. We just don't earn brownie points for doing them. We do them because we love Him, and we love Him because He loves us. But the extent of our love for Him is limited to the extent of our understanding and experience of His love for us.

If we do good works simply to earn brownie points, we cancel grace. Can anything be shallower than loving God for what we can get out of Him? Let's be honest, ulterior motives and hidden agendas don't make for genuine relationships.

So, if we cannot earn His favour, how should we go about obtaining it? It's a whole lot simpler than we could ever imagine! It's available through faith—nothing more (Gal 5:4). Afterall, grace can only be granted when it is not deserved!

On the road to gaining an understanding of grace, there were concepts that I found difficult to embrace. At times my legalistic upbringing would get in the way, causing me to doubt the concepts that had so excited me. Let's face it, it's not easy to forsake a lifetime's indoctrination.

The message of grace, and the more popular message of "works plus grace", expounded Sunday after Sunday, are poles apart. But what so many don't seem to understand, is that a mixture of contradictory concepts make both unworkable! The one cancels the other—rendering each strategy useless! Galatians 5:4 says, *"If you are trying to make yourself right with God by keeping the law, you have been cut off from Christ! You have fallen away from God's grace"* (NLT).

That's pretty plain isn't it? According to this scripture grace is not an optional way. Any other way severs our connection with God's Son and His grace. Without His grace we have nothing more than Islam or one of the other world religions. Grace is what sets Christianity apart—it does not feature in any other world religion.

Most of us will be familiar with the scripture, *"'Not by might, not by power, but by My Spirit' says the Lord of hosts".* (Zechariah 4:6 KJV). This is a very strong grace scripture. Read the next verse, *"Who art thou, O great mountain? Before Zerubbabel thou shalt become a plain: and he shall bring forth the headstone thereof with shoutings, crying, grace, grace unto it".*

Zerubbabel was facing insurmountable obstacles with the rebuilding of the Temple—he was facing a mountain. What was the advice from the angel of the Lord? He was to shout *"grace, grace"* to the mountain, and it would become a plain. In other words, he was to depend upon the strength of God and not upon the arm of the flesh to move the mountain. Of course, Zerubbabel was incapable of moving mountains; fortunately, there was a better way, and that way was grace. With grace God would do it for him!

There are things in our lives that we are incapable of handling on our own, no matter how much effort we may exert. One is that we are incapable of truly transforming ourselves. That is something that can only be achieved by grace. God is saying that we are to cry *"grace, grace"* to our personal mountains of sinful habits and behavioural issues beyond our control.

As you embark on this journey, like me, you may encounter many naysayers and religious sceptics along the way. I have discovered that God is good, and that He Himself has already made a way to empower us to live above sin. He has also made a way for us to enter into our full inheritances while still on the Planet. We are not required to make ourselves perfect. Even if we could, it would not be enough to impress God. It is only by inheritance through faith that we obtain anything from Him; not by reward for religious endeavours.

But beware! In your enquiries, you are likely to encounter well-meaning theologians who will refute the idea that God's favour is unconditional. Kindly churchmen will endeavour to keep you performing—always having to impress God in the hope that He will notice your piety and favour you for it. And then when nothing happens, you will be encouraged to soldier on in the hope that your added strivings will eventually payoff. But inheritances are gifts; not rewards. Though sincerely well meant, these mentors succeed only in disinheriting us.

Jesus warned us of this error when he told us to beware of the leaven of the Pharisees. Jews were not permitted to eat leavened bread. Even the tiniest addition of yeast has a way of permeating into the whole loaf of bread. In the same way, even the slightest addition of law will permeate its way into grace, thus cancelling it altogether. In God's economy, it has to be grace and grace alone, without the slightest hint of Old Testament law keeping.

Be on your guard—naysayers are a plenty! The story of grace cannot be reasoned; it can only be received by divine revelation. Look to Him for a revelation of His good intensions towards you. Do not allow yourself to be drawn back into the burden of fulfilling "*the law of sin and death*".

I have put this down on paper to help anyone who would want to participate in God's goodness. I trust that these simple explanations will help you discover the favour He wants you to have—His love for you is intense—way beyond your wildest dreams!

38

THE LOVE STORY

Love stories are two a penny—few are memorable, but at least one has stood the test of time. It was told by the greatest fiction storyteller of all times. At the top of his list of best sellers is the story of the black sheep of the family returning home to a mixed reception. This story is better known as the "parable of the prodigal son" (Luke 15:11-32).

Jesus used fiction to mirror real life. His stories were not frivolous—each one contains hidden nuggets of divine revelation. To this day, we continue to uncover layers of hidden wisdom.

This is a story of a rebellious son's return home, and a loving father's unconditional forgiveness. This is also the story of the older brother's misunderstanding of how to go about obtaining his father's approval.

How would the older brother have told this story? Allow me to tell a parable of a parable.

The Parable

This is the story of Mr Goody Two-Shoes. Goody was a model son in the Two-Shoes household. As the eldest son, he was ever so careful not to do anything that could possibly tarnish the Two-Shoes family name. Whenever his father needed anything done, he would be the first to volunteer. As the prime heir to the family fortune, his father's approval was important. For this reason, he was always prepared to go the extra mile and do more than his fair share, avoiding anything untoward, lest he disqualify his inheritance. He worked every bit as hard as any of the servants, doing whatever it took to stay in his father's good books.

In all, he was a model son; admired by all for his diligence and commitment to family matters.

His younger brother, "Nearly-Good Two-Shoes", also did his best to please his dad. Unfortunately, he was always outdone by his older brother, who was never shy to tell him that his efforts were not meeting with family expectations. After many years of being overshadowed and outdone by Goody, he concluded that he would never be able to measure up, so he asked his father for his inheritance and shipped out. He wasn't a bad boy; he just suffered from an inferiority complex— always being put down by his older brother who was never shy to voice his disapproval.

The family heard nothing from Nearly-Good for some years. When word eventually came, it wasn't at all good. Nearly-Good had brought dishonour to the family name. Goody was not at all surprised to hear this. It only confirmed what he had always believed about the black sheep of the family. His vagabond brother was up to no good, living it up with all manner of hedonism and debauchery. Later, when Goody got more news, it was that Nearly-Good had blown his entire inheritance and fallen on hard times. Goody secretly rejoiced, and even gloated over his brother's misfortune. "At last, he had gotten his just desserts for dragging the family name through the mud". Goody had always believed that Nearly-Good would never learn anything unless it came to him the hard way.

One day, after a particularly hard day's work, as Goody was coming home from the fields, he heard the sounds of celebrations. He asked the servants what all the carousing was about, and was told that his brother had returned home, and that his father had killed the fatted calf to celebrate his return. Taken aback by the news—concluding that his father must have been suckered in by this sorry looser? He wouldn't put anything past the slacker. How could his dad possibly be pleased to have his name publicly linked to this miserable bum?

As Goody came upon the celebration, he was stunned by the honour his dad was bestowing upon Nearly-Good. The scoundrel was wearing his father's sandals, ring and robe over a filthy body that stank of body odour and pigswill. "Surely he deserved to be punished for the disgrace he had brought upon the family name!" Goody blurted out, *"Look! All these years I've been slaving for you and never disobeyed your orders. Yet you never gave me even a young goat so I could celebrate with my friends. But when this son of yours who has squandered your property with prostitutes comes home, you kill the fattened calf for him!"* (Luke 15:29,30 NIV)

Who is the Older Brother?

It is only natural to identify with the prodigal. All of us have veered, if only slightly, from the path at some time in our Christian walk. Our best shot at living right has let us down—we have fallen short of our heavenly Father's impeccable character.

But for a moment, put yourself in the boots of the older brother. I think it is safe to say that we have all tried to get God's attention through good deeds and law keeping—prepared to do whatever it takes to gain His favour. We had hoped that our good deeds and law keeping would be noticed and counted as proof of devotion, and that it would shift us up a notch or two above the rank and file of average "pew warmers".

And to top it all, we may have gone out of our way to impress our brothers and sisters with our holiness—a well-used tactic to gain respect.

Sadly, law keeping has a way of elevating a person. But let's face it— haughtiness is not at all pretty. Before we know it, we are looking down our noses at those who are failing to live up to our religious attainments.

If you are finding it difficult to identify with the older brother, take a moment to consider your motives for striving to please God. I don't think I would be wrong in saying that we have all had older brother mentality at some point in our Christian walk. To be frank, older brother smugness is pretty much typical of contemporary Christianity.

Older brother thinking is the very thing that makes us, the church, distasteful to the world. How did we sink to this level? Quite simply— the devil hoodwinked us into believing that the benefits of Jesus' "Last Will and Testament" are conditional—dispersed to beneficiaries in accordance with Christian performance. We are led to believe that we cannot benefit from the "Last Will and Testament" unless our actions comply with the conditions of a previous testament. But the bottom line is that rules pertaining to pervious testaments have no bearing on current testaments.

If, by some chance, we manage to keep some law, we are likely to look with disdain upon those who are less able—it's a malady common to all humanity. Actually, if God favoured us for our law keeping, we would all be in big trouble! If no-one in the history of mankind has ever managed to do enough, then it is obvious that His favour cannot be obtained in this way.

We may confidently say that we do not break any of the Ten Commandments, but if we have ever been angry with anyone, Jesus said that we are every bit as guilty as a murderer. The devil knows this, so in order to distract us from finding true godliness through grace, all he needs to do is to keep us trying to fulfil the law. But like little puppies, no matter how hard we may try to catch our tails, it is just not going to happen.

The law demands perfection, something humanity is incapable of achieving! If we fail to keep one Old Covenant commandment, we are held guilty of all ten commandments. Clearly, the odds are stacked against us—nobody could possibly inherit on this basis, period! Galatians 3:10 (NIV) says, 'All who rely on observing the law are under a curse, for it is written: "Cursed is everyone who does not continue to do everything written in the Book of the Law."' Clearly no-one is capable of keeping every last law, and therefore, no-one can obtain justification in this way. Thankfully, God has provided us with a way that is attainable— "The righteous will live by faith" (Gal 3:11 NIV). It is by faith alone—there is simply no other way to obtain righteousness.

So long as Satan can keep us working to gain inheritances, he can keep us out of our inheritances. If it were remotely possible to inherit by reward, then it would no longer be by bequest. The New Testament is an outright bequest. Bequests by their very nature are free—they simply cannot be earned!

In the parable of the prodigal son, everything that belonged to the father, belonged to the older brother. Even fatted calves belonged to him. He could have killed any number of fatted calves and have thrown any number of parties, yet he mistakenly thought that he had to earn the right to do so. For as long as he expected to inherit by reward, he was unable to inherit by free bequest.

Are we Servants or Sons?

When Goody expressed his disgust, his father replied, *"My son, you are always with me, and everything I have is yours"* (Luke 15:31 NIV).

Goody was confused between the two roles played out in the Two-Shoes household. There were servants and there were sons. Servants were rewarded with wages. Sons co-owned all through inheritance. In evaluating himself in terms of his performance, he missed the point—nobody can earn what they already own. In his own words, *"Look! All these years I've been slaving for you and never disobeyed your orders. Yet you never gave me even a young goat so I could celebrate with my friends"* (Luke 15:29,30 NIV). He was under the mistaken impression that he must earn favour. He obviously did not understand that he was already in his Father's favour; not by reason of his performance, but by reason of a covenant that fathers' have with their children! For son's, there is no place for servant thinking—servant's wages were paid from family assets. If he were to be rewarded, he would have to pay his own money to himself. Why on earth would he do that? As insane as this may sound, it is nevertheless a concept often taught from pulpits. But as recipients of vast inheritances, rewards are of no interest to us.

If we regard ourselves to be servants, we are likely to measure our performance against fellow servants' performances. Sadly, achievements lead to pride, and before we know it, we, like Goody, are judging others for not measuring up to our standards.

In the Two-Shoes household, servants lived in servant's quarters. No matter how comfortable they may have been, servant's quarters were no match for the opulent luxury of the palatial homestead.

The father had a good relationship with his servants, but he never put his arms around them and kissed them, as he often did with his sons. Even a handshake was rare for the servants.

The father was good to the servants and rewarded them for going the extra mile, but he never surprised them with gifts for absolutely no reason at all, as he often did for his sons.

From time to time, the father would fire unproductive servants, but never once fired unproductive sons. Instead, he threw a party for a disgraced son! The father did not tolerate misbehaviour in the servant's quarters, but had oodles of patience, forgiveness and love for misbehaving sons. Not even the awful disgrace of squandering the family fortune and bringing shame upon their noble name, was enough to change his decision to love his delinquent son.

Are we Servants of God? Jesus said, *"I no longer call you servants"* (John 15:15 NIV). We are not servants of God; we are His sons and daughters. As children we choose to serve Him, but we are not classified as servants who earn wages. Why would we be interested in wages when we are already in receipt of an immense inheritance? Blessings are not rewards; they are bequests gratuitously bestowed upon us for no reason other than that we, as children of a generous

Papa, are immensely loved. We do not serve Him to be favoured, but rather serve Him because we are favoured—serving out of love, rather than duty.

As New Covenant believers, we are not looking for rewards; the estate has already been apportioned in accordance with the Testator's wishes. Either we grasp this concept, or we don't! If not, we simply forgo indulging in the abundant generosity of a loving Father. We share everything with Him, I mean everything! Jesus doesn't own a penny more than the weakest most immature believer alive today. Favouring us is not dependant on our Father's whims and fancies— He has already made up His mind and bundled everything we could ever wish for into His "Last Will and Testament". It is up to us to either indulge in or fail to indulge in His generosity. The choice is entirely ours! Extravagant favour awaits those who understand what He has so bountifully conferred upon us!

Rewards belong to the Old Covenant. In that covenant, law keeping was rewarded. Under the New Testament, Jesus fulfilled the laws and all the conditions of the Old Covenant on our behalf, thereby removing this burden from our shoulders. We often have difficulty getting our minds around such a liberating concept, but understanding it is vital to our spiritual wellbeing, without which we end up needlessly striving for stuff that cannot be rewarded. The good news is that faith completely negates the need for religious striving!

What about the principal of sowing and reaping? Is this not a New Covenant service that invokes a reward? No! It is not a reward; it is the multiplication of seed through the covenant of sowing and reaping. This covenant was initiated long before the Law of Moses and remains in force by faith alone; it is not a reward for service; it is a harvest for sowing.

Different Approaches; Different Results

Let's look at the contrasting outcomes of the two brothers in the parable of the prodigal son:

Older brother	Prodigal son
Disciplined living	Riotous living
Obedience	Disobedience
Faithful in service	Absconded from service
Faithful to his father	Deserted his father
Carried out his duties	Abandoned his duties
Self-confidence	No confidence in his flesh
Pride in personal accomplishments	Humility, having no accomplishments of which to boast
Worked to be rewarded	Did nothing to be rewarded
Missed out on his father's favour	Endowed with his father's favour

Sadly, much of the church has older brother mentality. Is it any wonder that the church has lost its salty savour to attract the world to our Saviour? The older brother meets us at the church door with pepper (judgemental attitude) to irritate our eyes, instead of salt (unconditional love) to tantalize our taste buds.

If church is really all that it is cracked up to be, why do so many of its members prefer the beach, TV and sport? Sure, there are those who dutifully never miss a service, but can God really feel loved when love is given out of duty? Surely love is only truly love when it is given without reason!

I can just imagine how delighted God must be to receive our service when we are delighted to serve Him—when we love Him for no other reason than that He loves us. But can He possibly feel the same when we are buttering Him up for favours. As with anyone, I am sure that He appreciates sincerity. Clearly, love is only truly love when it comes without strings attached?

Which would you prefer of your marriage partner? An attitude of, "He or she loves me because he or she must", or "He or she loves me because he or she loves me". Similarly with God—He is not impressed with our grin and bear it church attendance, nor is He impressed with our grin and bear it Christian service. In God's book, only actions that are heartfelt count as worship. When we discover how unconditionally we are loved, "genuine" worship soon follows.

Only One Payment Due

The question remains, are we indebted to Jesus for the tremendous sacrifice He made for our benefit? Afterall, nobody has ever done as much for us. The price He paid was enormous, to say the least! How do we even begin to explain that, as undeserving as we are, we are nevertheless loved and blessed beyond human reason? If His blessings were given to indebt us to Him, what a huge burden we would have to shoulder. All of humanity combined does not possess nearly enough resources to repay the enormous price Jesus paid for our right standing with His Father. Any endeavour to repay the favour, would consign us to lifelong futility. We would be taking on a task that simply cannot be completed. But thankfully, we are not expected to turn blessings into debts. Jesus came to do the precise opposite—He turned debts into credits, and curses into blessings. The debtor's ethic is life sapping—a price too high for mortals!

The good news is that we do not owe Jesus a penny. There was only one payment God required for our sinfulness, and Jesus' settled in full! The price was the pristine blood of the sinless Lamb of God. Even if God were to grant us a lifetime repayment plan, nobody could possibly live nearly long enough to settle the debt. He found somebody else, His very own Son, Jesus, to stand in for us, making one grand payment in full and final settlement.

If, before rebirth, we could not buy our way into heaven, what makes us think that we could possibly buy a right to remain in good standing with God. If we couldn't repay Jesus before rebirth, it's not going to happen after rebirth. Our good works fell horribly short then, and still fall horribly short now. Either Jesus did it all, or we are in serious trouble! Besides, His blood payment was a gift, and as long as we don't try to repay it, it remains entirely free!

The price He paid for the gift was so high, that to try to repay it would trivialise it; reducing its value to the sum-total of our pitiful efforts—hardly a fraction of the price He paid. Furthermore, any attempt to pay for a gift is an insult to the giver—it reduces a gesture of love to that of a purchase. How ungracious it would be of us to reduce His glorious gift to nothing more than a business obligation— a payment for services rendered. Thankfully, He takes pleasure in lavishing gifts upon us without any thought of indebting us.

Repayments do not count as worship. Worship is infatuation—not something done by compulsion, nor something done to obligate Him to favour us. It's a declaration of love—a desire to bring pleasure to Him!

There is a special kind of joy in receiving something from someone who really cares for us. Rather than trying to repay something that isn't owed, let us give to Him in the same spirit that He gives to us—love without hidden agendas.

"So what", you might be thinking. "Does it really matter whether I am repaying a debt or giving a love gift"? It matters much, because God says that we are not to give under compulsion, but to give joyfully out of free will. So often money is casually slipped onto offering plates without giving it so much as a second thought. This is a lost opportunity—it could just as easily be a precious gesture of heartfelt worship.

By repaying a debt, we are effectively stooping to something that Jesus' blood rendered obsolete. Striving to fulfilling Old Testament obligations, is all it takes to cancel New Testament privileges.

From God's eternal perspective, long before we were born, He looked ahead through the ages and viewed our entire lives in advance. He not only saw each and every sin that we would commit before our salvation; He also saw each and every sin we would commit after receiving salvation. Despite knowing all this, He still went to the cross for us.

The question arises—did He die for our pre-salvation sins, or for our post salvation sins? On the cross, when He said, *"It is finished"*, He truly meant what he said. He had made payment in full and final settlement for all our sins, even the ones we are yet to commit. Oh, what a magnificent gift! What a glorious Saviour! How can we help but feel deeply indebted? Yet we owe Him not a penny!

BEWITCHED CHRISTIANS

Goody Two-Shoes and ourselves are not the only ones to be bewitched into thinking that our inheritances can be earned. Paul wrote, *"You foolish Galatians! Who has bewitched you?... Are you so foolish? After beginning with the Spirit, are you now trying to attain your goal by human effort?"* (Gal 3:1,3 NIV)

The church sometimes says that we are saved by grace alone, but then goes on to say that we need more than grace to stay saved—we need works. This is the same error that the Galatians had fallen into. Paul also wrote, *"As you have therefore received Christ Jesus the Lord, so walk in Him"* (Col 2:6 NKJV). How did we receive Him? Was it by the good works we had done? Or was it by grace through faith? In view of our faulty efforts, it couldn't be more obvious, it had to be by grace through faith alone! If that's how we got saved, then let's not change the rules now that we are saved—let's continue walking in him, with nothing more than faith, without a single credit to our names.

How does the enemy bewitch us? It's a simple matter. He does not have to get us to commit some atrocious sin. All he has to do is to convince us to add one tiny law to grace, and we are hexed—bewitched by the thought that we can earn God's favour.

What is the outcome of this bewitchment? Our sincerest attempts to gain God's favour through law keeping, serve only to cancel grace—

law keeping and grace are diametrically opposite. We do not gain blessings through law keeping; we gain curses—the very same curses from which we were saved.

He calls the kind of righteousness that comes through self-effort *"filthy rags"*. The kind of right living that He offers through a divinely changed heart is different—it is uncontaminated by flawed self-effort. It pleases the enemy when we try to obtain God's favour through law-keeping—it's how he keeps our inheritances out of reach.

It seems wrong doesn't it? Some of us have been so conditioned by well-meant sermons that it is difficult to believe that it is not our piety, but our childlike faith that gives us access to heaven's provisions—inheritances are entirely free of charge!

We have been living by this weird and wonderful idea that God's favour only goes to those who deserve it. So we do our best to master our flesh—a commendable but unachievable task. Never in the history of mankind has any person attained perfection, and God's standard is nothing short of perfection. If we insist on pursuing the attainment of worthiness, the enemy will keep us bewitched and imprisoned in a sense of guilt and unworthiness. Seeking God's favour in this way is the ultimate wild goose chase!

Qualification for Grace

What qualifies us for God's grace? Is it our holiness, our love, our kindness, our faithfulness, our goodness, our fruitfulness or maybe the purity of our living? It is none of the above. Really? In that case how do we qualify? Relax! Jesus has fully qualified us without our assistance. If that is so, why are some more blessed than others? What is the secret to receiving God's favour? It is faith! Surely it couldn't be that simple? Oh yes it is! It is nothing more than a matter of expressing our faith in a gracious Father—a Father who has committed Himself by covenant to bless His beloved children.

A covenant obligates the parties to it to carry out its terms and conditions. Just in case we are not entirely convinced, He validated it with a signature signed in the blood of His only begotten Son. What more proof of commitment could we ask for? His promises are yea and amen! All He expects of us, is that we receive what He so graciously obtained for us. All it takes are words declared in faith!

Most Christians are not convinced of this, and consequently consign themselves to a life sentence of slaving for approval—forever floundering for favour. Sadly, disillusionment is their only reward. Grace simply cannot be obtained through any amount of striving.

If we could gain holiness through religious striving, there would be no need for grace. God's favour would simply be measured to us in line with our efforts. But rewards bear no resemble to grace. In fact, rewards are the precise antithesis of grace. No need to work for Kingdom rewards when inheritances are ready and waiting to be collected. Grace bears no charge—it is received by faith!

You are not the only one having difficulty accepting that it could possibly be this easy. Our religious paradigms have been drummed into our heads over years of faithful church attendance. The world operates on rewards and retributions. Society has conditioned us to believe that good service deserves compensation, and that injustices deserve punishment. It's not easy to grasp concepts that run contrary to social norms.

The world has little patience for repeat offenders. On rare occasions, a person may be given a second chance, but there is a limit to what will be tolerated. When we break a person's trust, we lose credibility! Friends will not stand for it, and customers, even less. But these concepts are far removed from the kingdom of God, far removed from grace!

When believers fall into gross sin, should they be allowed to continue fellowshipping? Religion requires that indiscretions be disciplined. Grace is simply put aside as religious indignation is expressed in "righteous" outrage. When a person of prominence falls, he is forced to step down from ministry, and in some cases, ostracised or obliged to submit to the rod of church discipline.

I know of one who committed adultery with a trusted member's wife. And if that wasn't immoral enough, he went on to murder her husband. Would you allow him back into ministry? Would you seek his counsel for your marriage? Would you even trust him with your wife?

Another landed up with his wife in a strange town in a place he should not have gone to. When he realised that they were in trouble with the wrong crowd, he knew he would have to come up with something to save his neck. So, he told his wife to play along and let them do whatever they wanted with her. He waited while they violated her. Tell me, would you trust him in ministry? What is worse, he got into the same kind of trouble a second time and again used his wife to save his neck.

Another very prominent minister publicly denied Christ. Would you trust him behind a pulpit?

All three of these men subsequently became spiritual giants in the kingdom. Isn't the grace of God just so amazing? God used these men to change the world. Their names were King David, Abraham and Peter.

There were more—Jacob, Moses and many others—deceivers, connivers, murderers and the like. They all went on to be honoured and highly favoured by God. Isn't His grace wonderful?

Thankfully, the only thing that qualifies us for God's grace is our faith. From God's side, the blood covenant is complete—there is nothing more for Him to do. When He declared, *"it is finished"*, payment had been made in full and final settlement for all time and eternity. Consequently, inheritances may be claimed without charge—all that's required of us is simple faith!

God can deal with our failures, but He cannot work with self-sufficiency. With self-sufficiency we don't need any help from God—it's all about us and our achievements—plain and simply religious pride! Sadly, our achievements give us reason to judge those who are less able to achieve what we have managed to achieve. If we insist on achieving holiness by self-effort, God will not interfere. The older brother, Goody Two-Shoes, honestly believed that it was by his efforts that he had gained favour with his father. Sadly, he ended up disillusioned, jealous, bitter and twisted.

Humanism

Some preachers urge their flocks to straighten out their lives. Sounds pious enough. But is it really the gospel of our Lord Jesus? No, not even close! It is as far removed from the gospel as we can get—precisely opposite to His grace. The burden that religion has placed upon our shoulders simply cannot be borne by mortals.

If we are required to change ourselves, we have nothing but humanism with which to accomplish it. Whether churched or unchurched, anyone can undertake human effort. We do not need God or His Holy Spirit to operate in humanism. In fact, humanism by its very nature specifically excludes God.

Although humanism is Satan's counterfeit religion, it is one of the most widely taught doctrines in Christianity—the doctrine of "holiness" by behavioural modification. When confronting this devilish doctrine, Isaiah came close to using profanity in His criticism of it—calling it the doctrine of filthy menstruation rags. In the culture of the day, this was one of the lowest insults that one could express without actually cursing. Paul used equally derogatory language when he described his own righteousness as dung!

God's grace poses the biggest threat to Satan's skulduggery, and that's why He uses religious humanism—he will do anything to undermine God's grace. Let's settle this once and for all—religion bears absolutely no resemblance to God's grace, period! Religion is what Jesus came to put a decisive end to—humanity is absolutely powerless of sanctifying itself.

We are often encouraged to clean up our acts. We respond by doing our best to modify our behaviour. But nobody can accomplish what can only be accomplished by the love of God. Religious humanism is anathema—foreign to the gospel of our Lord Jesus!

We all have our own brand of hang-ups. For instance, believers who have an anger problem may learn to restrain their tempers. But that's not God's way—it's the way of the flesh. Besides, it does not solve the problem; it simply drives anger inwards, where it is left to fester unseen.

So many have resigned themselves to the endless futility of repeatedly repenting of the same iniquity without the slightest chance of gaining enduring victory. To be perfectly frank, religious humanism has no place in Christianity!

Wouldn't it be great if we could end the cycle of repeatedly having to repent of the same sins without any hope of victory? Endless striving is wearing us out! Is victory by effort even remotely possible? Certainly not! But thankfully, with grace it is gloriously possible! No need to keep our flesh in check—rather repent towards God. Repenting "from" sin requires disciplined restraint, whereas repenting "towards God" requires no restraint—it is not we, but He who assumes responsibility for conquering our iniquities.

With changed hearts, we simply have no appetite for the iniquities that had plagued us. Grace empowers us to make quality choices. Let's not beat about the bush. Anything short of unconditional love does not possess the power to change a person for the better.

When we begin to value ourselves in the way that God does, who cares that religious people think less of us! We are able to be ourselves regardless. Let's face it, He is in love with us; not with the person we pretend to be.

I saw a classic adage displayed in a coffee shop. Painted boldly across a wall were the profound words, "Be yourself—everybody else is taken". These classic words would not be out of place above the lintels of church doors.

Sadly, when rules fail to change hearts, religious pretence is sure to follow. Though pretence makes nonsense of a person's religion, it's quite acceptable when everybody else is also pretending. But once awakened to God's undying love for us, what could religious approval possibly add? Our past religious pretending becomes nothing more than a cause of embarrassment!

The bottom line is: Whilst being transformed by the value our Father bestows upon us, there is no need to be religiously controlled. No need to demand holiness of us; it follows without persuasion!

Does this mean that we will never fall again? Wouldn't that be wonderful? No! Although sanctification is complete in God's mind, it takes time for it to filter through our hearts into our actions—it's not an event; it's a process! We need more than a lifetime to turn all our weaknesses over to God.

It is so easy to cross the line from grace into humanism. It is accidentally taught by well-meaning preachers who have no ulterior motives—they sincerely desire that their flocks forsake un-Christ-likeness. But righteousness simply cannot be attained by any amount of striving. If God regards our very best strivings as *"filthy rags"*, then better that we stop striving. Fortunately, entitlement to kingdom privileges does not rely upon strivings; it relies upon the terms and conditions of Jesus' "Last Will and Testament". It is not a matter of obligating God; He has already obligated Himself to abide by the terms of an unbreakable Covenant—it is all about grace! Divine inheritances are not appropriated in accordance with piety; they are appropriated in accordance with faith!

Satan is not against good moral living. In fact, he encourages it. As long as he can keep Christians trying to achieve a good moral lifestyle, he knows that they will not see the need to look to God for His ongoing process of sanctification. Afterall, Satan knows only too well that nothing divine can be achieved by self-effort. It doesn't concern him in the least bit that they may achieve a form of godliness—he knows that a form of godliness will deny the power thereof. Self-righteous making is a gazillion miles short of holiness!

Look at the world's view on morality. They genuinely believe that their morals are higher than God's. Afterall, they feel that God is morally deficient because He is against abortion. "How could a loving God give more value to a foreign growth in a womb, than to a woman's convenience?" they may ask. While they refuse to regard a foetus as a defenceless child, they avoid facing up to the reality of child murder. This distorted view on morality is a clear example of what happens when God is left out of the equation.

Before we claim that our morals will never be in disagreement with God's, and that we would never be guilty of such blatant distortions, don't forget that our best moral living still falls hopelessly short of the glory of God.

We need God's open-heart surgery, without which we remain enslaved to our appetites for sin. Satan does not want us to know this—he keeps it from us—keeping us preoccupied with the distraction of striving to live good moral lives.

Grace plus Lifestyle

Your boat sank in the middle of the ocean. Moments before possibly drowning, you were found and rescued by helicopter. No sooner were you airlifted, than your rescuers tossed you out of the helicopter, telling you to swim a thousand kilometres home in the same turbulent seas from which you had just been rescued.

Sound ridiculous? Of course it is! Yet it is often the fate of believers. We are taught that we are saved by grace alone (the helicopter), because nobody can save themselves. Now that we are saved, we are expected to keep our salvation by changing our lifestyles (we are returned to the same treacherous waters from which were saved, expected to make it back on our own). In other words, it is claimed that it takes grace alone to save us, but a lot more than grace to keep us saved.

Verses like, God requires us to work out our salvation with fear and trembling, are often quoted. Please note that He does not require us to work for our salvation; He requires us to work our salvation out. In other words, we are to live in the victory that was accomplished on the cross. We are not saved "by" good works; we are saved "unto" good works. Although we do not work for grace; grace inspires us to do the works of Jesus!

If we are saved by grace, but not kept saved by grace, then we must concede, we are very sorry individuals. Our salvation hangs on a very fragile thread. Our works, being the weakest link, make our salvation tenuous at best! Could we even imagine a responsible God entrusting the fickle behaviour of humanity with the responsibility of keeping themselves saved? Surely He knows us better than that! For that matter we know ourselves better than that. Here is the good news! God didn't create a flimsy plan of salvation. Either our salvation stands on the solid rock, Christ Jesus, or it does not stand at all!

"As you have therefore received Christ Jesus the Lord, so walk in Him", (Col 2:6 NKJV). We were saved when we responded in faith to God's grace. He did not require any assistance from us—not even a single good work to commend ourselves. Now, in the same way, we are to allow God's gracious Spirit to continue to keep us. He is not looking for human assistance; He is looking for human co-operation! When we try to change ourselves, we interfere with His divine process of changing us from within. We need to stay in the helicopter of grace, without which we will drown. Our weak efforts cannot do it—nobody

can make it on their own in the turbulence of an angry ocean; we must continue to rely upon grace and grace alone!

Thankfully, we are not expected to take on the mammoth task of holy making—it is something that God has committed to do for us— he wants to take us from glory to glory. It happens when we allow Christ within us, to emit His light, love and righteousness through us (2Cor 3:18). We are drawn into this relationship with agape love.

When judgement is removed from the equation, romance has every opportunity to blossom and bloom. Although we are inherently flawed and faulty, we are nevertheless perfectly understood—our weaknesses don't even get a mention. Is there any wonder that we find ourselves submitting to His tender caresses without persuasion—His kind of grace is immensely appealing?

While we are of the opinion that God judges us, we are likely to fall into the trap of striving to gain His favour. To achieve this, we'll most likely attempt to modify our behaviour. But no matter how gallant our efforts may be, this strategy achieves naught. As sad as it is to say, our sincerest efforts leave us floundering in futility. For our trouble, we don't get holiness; we get self-righteousness—not something that would impress a holy God! We simply cannot swim home on our own—we will drown. We dare not leave the rescue helicopter—we dare not leave grace!

When God changes us, He always works from the inside outwards, and never from the outside inwards. To do so, He influences us with nothing more than undeserved love. Clearly, only hearts captured by His love can be transformed by His love.

"Not by might nor by power but by My Spirit says the Lord of hosts". (Zechariah 4:6 NKJV) We have a choice, either to attempt to change ourselves by our own might and power, or to be changed by His love

and the power of His Spirit. Both ways are productive. The one produces hypocrisy, in the form of filthy rags; while the other produces holiness, in the form of fruit of the Spirit. By taking on the task of modifying our behaviour, we forfeit the privilege of being transformed by love.

In view of these two outcomes, perhaps we should work backwards. First decide on the desired outcome (filthy rags or sanctification), and then consider what causes these outcomes. Filthy rags are produced by trying to change ourselves, while sanctification is produced by allowing His gracious love to transform us from within.

The Fruit of the Spirit

So many sermons call upon us to display love, joy, peace, longsuffering, kindness, goodness, faithfulness, gentleness and self-control. Unfortunately, when we feel obliged to make this happen, the burden of change rests upon us. For merely trying to produce this gorgeous fruit, we end up with something that is nauseating to God.

It is not the farmer who decides what type of fruit a tree will produce; trees produce after their own kind. In the same way, we cannot tell our flesh to produce something that can only be produced by the Spirit—flesh can only produce works of the flesh.

How then can we produce these wonderful character traits? The Spirit, like a tree, produces what it intrinsically is—apple trees produce apples and peach trees produce peaches. How do we avoid the trap of producing fleshly fruit? *"But when the Holy Spirit controls our lives, He will produce this kind of fruit in us: love, joy, peace, patience, kindness, goodness, faithfulness, gentleness, and self-control"* (Gal 5:22 NLT). Did you notice that He will produce His fruit; not us? The choice is simple: Either allow Him to produce His very own fruit through us, or attempt to force the issue by doing it ourselves. But counterfeit fruit remains counterfeit! Plastic smiles remain plastic smiles—far from real!

Fruit is not produced by the branches of the tree (our flesh); it is produced by the sap in the branches (the Holy Spirit within us). But a problem arises when we jump in to lend a helping hand to the Spirit. It's as though we don't trust Him to do what He said He would do.

"The law no longer holds you in its power, because you died to its power when you died with Christ on the cross. And now you are united with the one who was raised from the dead. As a result you can produce good fruit i.e. good deeds for God" (Rom 7:4 NLT).

A while back, there was a scam in South Africa. Cheap sunflower seed oil was packaged as top class cold pressed extra virgin olive oil. It looked the same, but it was counterfeit. Sunflower oil is bad for your health and has cancer risks; while olive oil is good for you and helps to prevent heart disease.

Our lives, like these bottles, may bear pretty Christian labels, and be of some use, yet contain something less than the Spirit's wonderful fruit. His fruit simply cannot be manufactured; it can only be produced by His Spirit—it requires nothing more than yielded-ness on our part.

Does the lack of fruit disqualify us from obtaining His favour? Not at all! Jesus never turned away a single unfruitful person who asked for His help. Unfruitfulness was never even an issue. All He needed to work with was a person's faith!

It was the pagan Centurion's faith, not his fruit that qualified him for God's favour. To add laws or conditions to grace is to cancel grace! Without grace there is no New Testament! And without the New Testament, we have no inheritance!

Just in case the Centurion's story is not convincing enough, it is interesting to note that both of Jesus' highest commendations for faith did not go to good honest law keepers, but to non-law keeping pagans. The other commendation went to a pagan Canaanite woman who refused to take no for an answer from Jesus. Jesus called her faith *"great"*. If Jesus gives more accolades to people of faith, who have no regard for Old Covenant law keeping, then perhaps we should be doing the same!

The Ark of the Covenant represented the presence of God. It had been left in the custody of Obededom. Its presence brought incredible blessings upon his family. Like Obededom, we have the presence of God. But unlike Obededom, we take His presence with us wherever we go—we are never without Him! Rebirth made us brand-new commodities blended with God Himself—our spirits combined with His Holy Spirit, unifying us into composite beings, unique and eternally indivisible!

A MISS IS AS GOOD AS A MILE

One of history's greatest scientific blunders was the multi-billion-dollar Hubbell, the world's most powerful telescope. After putting it into orbit, it was discovered that it could not focus anywhere nearly as well as my el-cheapo set of binoculars. The curvature of the telescope's vast lens was distorted by a lack of gravity in space. The designers had not factored these forces in. Thus, the project was rendered useless. The problem was eventually rectified at enormous expense, when astronauts placed something akin to a gigantic spectacle lens in front of the giant telescope. Suddenly everything came into perfect focus.

Everything that we see in life is viewed through lenses. Our eyes contain these lenses. If our lenses are distorted, then everything we see gets misinterpreted.

I have a condition known as astigmatism. My optometrist explained that our corneas should be curved like soccer balls. Unfortunately, mine are shaped like rugby balls—something like Bugs Bunny's eyes. This tends to distort images by elongating them. If both my rugby ball shaped corneas were perfectly aligned, I would be able to make more sense of what I see. Unfortunately, my left lens is like a rugby ball lying a few degrees to the right while my right lens is angled a few degrees to the left. To help me make sense of what I am looking at, he prescribed a lens for my left eye, to turn the image to the left, and a lens for my right eye, to turn the image to the right. Without the aid of my spectacles, I don't quite see what others see.

You and I may both be looking at the same image yet interpret it differently. It's not that reality is different; it's that our perception of reality is different.

My dad had cataracts removed from one eye, and later, from the other. After the first op, he was surprised to discover that curtains that he had thought to be green were actually blue. By closing one eye at a time, the curtains seemed to change from green to blue. Prior to the op, no one could have convinced him that they were actually blue.

Everybody has a different world-view. Our particular world-view is formed by our unique points of reference. Our interpretation on any matter is predetermined by the way we have experienced life, and everybody's experience is different. That being the case, it is vital to make sure that what we perceive on a particular matter, actually lines up with reality.

If we were flying at night without instruments to a tiny island 5000 kilometres away, and our direction was only one degree out to begin with, we would miss the island by many hundreds of kilometres. If our basics are wrong to start with, our conclusions will not only be wrong, they will be exaggerated into ever greater errors.

In the mid-seventies, our church discovered a new freedom that allowed us to drop some legalistic requirements such as dress codes and other lifestyle restrictions. We were told that this was because we had come into a better understanding of grace. Unfortunately, we continued to hold to the belief that we were under the guardianship of the law. This skewed our perceptions of God's goodness. I was under the mistaken impression that He would favour me if I behaved better. In all sincerity, I made an all-out attempt to change the way I behaved in hope of gaining His blessings.

This thinking gave me a warped understanding of His love. It led me to believe that His love, and therefore His favour, were for sale, an unfortunate perception that did nothing to bolster my confidence in prayer. How could I know whether my way of living was meeting with His approval? Fortunately, to withdraw grace by faith, has a vastly different outcome!

To be effective, faith must be convinced of the outcome—emphatic, confident, unshakable and expectant! Sadly, in the absence of these elements, prayers are rendered ineffective.

I have always been convinced that I was saved by grace alone, but I was not as convinced that I was doing enough to stay saved. I did my best to keep the Ten Commandments, and to stay on the right side of what my church expected of me. Unfortunately, like everybody else, I wasn't doing it all that well. Although I had moved away from some forms of legalism, I was still playing it safe by doing my best to deserve God's favour. I might not have been far off course when I set off for the island, but my error was increasingly exaggerated over time, to the extent that there was no possibility of reaching my intended destination.

As with a computer programme, our perceptions of reality are pre-programmed by the sum-total of our life's experiences. They predetermine the way we act and react.

In a world where there are no free lunches, we are likely to gain a slanted view of grace. For example; if our earthly fathers gave us less love when we misbehaved, then we are likely to expect the same from our heavenly Father. If Dad only showed us love when we deserved it, we will most likely expect the same treatment from our heavenly Dad. Sadly, if we believe that God's favour comes and goes in accordance with out holiness, we will miss grace by a country mile.

Although by definition, the undeserved favour of grace cannot be deserved, yet we do not automatically receive it. We must follow His instructions to get it. He has left us with a roadmap to guide us into His favour—it is called the Bible. It directs us to be in the right place at the right time to receive what He has made freely available to us.

He may cause a set of circumstances to playout in our favour, but we can't benefit from it unless we have followed His instructions to benefit from it. For example, He favours the humble but resists the proud. But then again, if you are under grace, you have absolutely nothing of which to boast—Jesus did it all!

Another problem with making the law our point of reference is that we will not only use it to measure ourselves; we will use it to measure others, thus falling into the awful ungraciousness of judgementalism!

If on the other hand, our reference point is mercy and grace, then the compassion we receive, becomes the compassion we spread. Our motivations are soon exposed. Judgementalism is evidence of law-keeping, while empathy is evidence of grace! If we view the world through the prism of the law, we unwittingly adopt judgementalism at a subconscious level. But if we view the world through the prism of grace, empathy follows without trying. With grace, everything about life takes on a different hue. Even the Bible seems to tell a different story—suddenly it all falls into place!

Before we were saved, we saw Christians as hypocrites. We couldn't help noticing that they weren't living up to their boast, even though we weren't doing much better ourselves. The day we got saved, Jesus gave us a new set of spectacles—they had a mercy and grace tint, similar to the ones He wears (metaphorically speaking). They gave us a new perspective on life.

This is what Jesus sees when He looks at us—we are beaming with His righteousness! He has a blind spot—refusing to notice our many sins. Let's be honest, even the saintliest of us are far from righteous in a practical sense. Thankfully, He has assured us that He doesn't impute or credit our sins to our account; He has already imputed them to Jesus' account (2Cor 5:19). He doesn't even make a mental note of them (Heb 8:12).

That being the case, how did we ever fall back into the nastiness of judging each other? Simple! Satan knows a very effective way to cause Christians to stumble. He doesn't have to get us into major sin. He simply tricks us into using the law to measure each other's actions—offence taking follows, and with it, Christianity's credibility is destroyed. He is not called the accuser of the brethren for nothing—accusations are his preferred tools of trade.

Many prefer judgement tinted spectacles—afterall, so much more can be seen, like the shortcomings and failures of fellow believers and leaders. Unfortunately, we also see our own failures and shortcomings, leading to feelings of unworthiness—enough to disinherit ourselves!

Jesus said, *"Judge not lest you be judged"*. As a consequence of judging others, we will be judged. On what basis will we be judged? When we judge others, whether by Old Testament law or by our church's legalism, we open ourselves to be judged by the very same laws we apply to others. And it doesn't take too long to find out that the Law's standards are unattainable—a discovery that leaves us with a sense of unworthiness—a faith debilitating, prayer nullifying condition!

Now, instead of God's mirror revealing our blood bought sinless children of God statuses, it reveals our alienated sinner statuses. The mirror is supposed to be the "perfect law of liberty", but when viewed through the "law of sin and death spectacles" we don't see our liberty; we see our bondage!

God's Mirror

"For if any be a hearer of the word, and not a doer, he is like unto a man beholding his natural face in a glass: For he beholdeth himself, and goeth his way, and straightway forgetteth what manner of man he was. But whoso looketh into the perfect law of liberty, and continueth therein, he being not a forgetful hearer, but a doer of the work, this man shall be blessed in his deed". (James 1:23-25 KJV)

A popular teaching on this scripture is that we are to look into the mirror of God's word to see our sinfulness and shortcomings, so that we know what needs fixing. But failings and shortcomings were not what God intended for us to discover in the mirror; it's our likeness to Him that He wants us to discover. It is our righteousness; not our unrighteousness that He wants to reveal to us by way of the mirror.

It's a fact of life: People become what they visualise of themselves. By visualising our sinfulness, we become more sinful. Conversely, by visualising our Christlikeness, we become more Christlike—His righteous becomes our way of life. Unfortunately, if we have been taught to see our unworthiness in the mirror, then the mirror serves only to perpetuate unworthiness. We may not know why, but we've been disinherited.

Human nature tends to act out the image it adopts of itself. As they say in the classics, "Give a dog a bad name"—a sure way to perpetuate anti-social behaviour.

The mirror is not about condemnation; the mirror is the image of Jesus—we are to see ourselves reflected in His image. Jesus is not only almighty God; He is also the prototype of every believer—the precise model of who we are. When we read about the magnificence of His glory, we are actually reading about the magnificence of ourselves.

Doesn't this give a whole new meaning to reading the scriptures? The story of Jesus is not only the story of a divine hero; it is the story of us, as victorious believers. That's you and me folks! He is the model of who you have become in Christ. The mirror reveals your personal righteousness in Him; seated together with Him in heavenly places; more than a conqueror; overcomer; devil beater; giant slayer; destined to win; blessed; the apple of His eye; heir and joint-heir together with Christ Jesus; anointed; healed; delivered and set free!

There can be no pleasure for God in seeing His children disinheriting themselves with an image far removed from the victorious image He wants them to adopt. He went to a lot of trouble to empower us to have so much more. If we look at ourselves in the mirror of the law of sin and death, it exposes our guilt and shame, and that's all it takes to engender feelings of unworthiness—enough to put God's favour out of reach!

Guess what the law of sin and death leads us into? The answer is exactly what its name suggests—we are led into sin and death! This is all that this law is capable of producing. God's desire for us is definitely not sin and death. Sin and death is what He came to save us from, replacing it with life, liberty and abundance.

When we go to the mirror of *"the perfect law of liberty"*, it is not our sinfulness that is revealed; it is our liberation from sinfulness. God has directed us to find freedom, liberty, and a Christ-like identity in the mirror.

What is *"the perfect law of liberty"*? Anybody attempting to keep *"the law of sin and death"* is cursed merely for trying, but *"the perfect law of liberty"* liberates us from every obligation and every curse listed in that Covenant. The Law of Moses can only make us conscience of our sins and shortcomings, whereas *"the perfect law of liberty"* makes us conscious of our right-standing with God.

Seeing that the New Covenant of grace was established for the purpose of liberating us from sin and its unfortunate consequences, it stands to reason that we should not be looking for our sinfulness in its reflection. That would be counterproductive—dragging us back into the very sins we were saved from. Sin is not what God would want us to discover about ourselves—His plan is redemptive, not anti-redemptive. But Satan's plan for us is very different. He uses a psychosis of failure to jeopardise faith! Unlike Satan, God desires that we nurture an image of unblemishable righteousness, every bit like Christ's—an image that leads to righteous living. Besides, faith thrives on a consciousness of right-standing.

Nothing fortifies faith more than unconditional love and acceptance, especially when it comes from God. Thankfully, in His eyes, we are entirely sinless!

Before we can expect to live in the victory of our Christlikeness, we may have to make some serious adjustments to our way of thinking. Afterall, we become exactly what we think of ourselves (Pro 23:7). Once Christ's image has been seared into our psyches, Christ-like actions follow without effort!

But we all, with open face beholding as in a glass (mirror) the glory of the Lord, are changed into the same image from glory to glory, even as by the Spirit of the Lord (2Co 3:18).

Once reborn, we need our perceptions of ourselves to be revolutionised in order to embrace what we have become. For that, the mirror reveals us as glorious new creations! With correct self-perceptions, a whole plethora of new possibilities arise.

"As He is, so are we in this world" (1John 4:17 KJV). Is Jesus glorious? Yes! So are we! Is He sinful? No! Neither are we! This knowledge affects the way we relate to God, which in turn, affects the way we rule and reign over life's challenges.

The more convinced we are of our similarity to Christ; the less appealing sin becomes—it simply loses its shine. If nothing intimidates Christ, then the same goes for us—there is no reason to allow anything to intimidate us. We are to come to the mirror to renew our minds—imprinting Christ's big image over our small picture of ourselves. With a victorious image, we are enabled to reign decisively, overcome convincingly, and complete our God given assignments with aplomb!

There is no need to strive to make ourselves right. The image we get of ourselves empowers us to deal with sin more effectively.

Just in case you are still not convinced that the mirror reveals our sinless-ness rather than our sinfulness, this scripture goes on to say that we are to look into the perfect law of liberty and *"continue therein"*. It is unconscionable to imagine that God would require us to continue in sin, and therefore it is obvious that the mirror does not reveal our sinfulness; it reveals our Christlikeness and right-standing with Him. If He wants us to continue doing what the mirror reveals, you can bet your bottom dollar that it reveals something superb!

What God wants us to see of ourselves in the mirror, is exactly what He sees in us. We know for a certainty that God does not see our sins. When He looks at us, He sees the righteousness He imputed to us.

Jerry Savelle said, "It is important to see yourself the way that God sees you so that you can believe that you can do what God says you can do and have what He says you can have". The mirror is meant to empower us to achieve the impossible, and to accomplish our God given assignments. God says that you are a champion. *"For the LORD does not see as man sees; for man looks at the outward appearance, but the LORD looks at the heart"* (1 Samuel 16:7b NKJV). No matter how weak and inadequate we may feel, we can always go to the mirror of Jesus to rediscover that we are up to the task, and more than able to overcome whatever obstacles we may encounter.

We have been invited to boldly enter the throne room of grace to find mercy and grace in our time of need. "The perfect law of liberty spectacles" are the only specs that should be worn in this room. If we insist on entering this room wearing the spectacles of "the law of sin and death", our perspective of our right-standing becomes distorted by our inability to meet its perfect standard—and that's all it takes to dismantle our faith. Wavering faith leaves lives spiritually powerless and prayers ineffective.

We cannot benefit from grace while we are attempting to make ourselves right with law keeping. Don't be deceived: Law cancels grace!

God's word settles this question once and for all. We are already the righteousness of God in Christ. We are already seated together with Christ Jesus in heavenly places. We are already brand-new creatures that never existed before, without any possibility of being tainted by sin for all time and eternity (2Cor 5:19).

If this is the description of a born-again believer, why do we continue sinning? The answer is that our minds remain susceptible—temptation comes via our five senses. If sin cannot take place in our eternally sinless spirits, where does it take place? It takes place in our minds (souls). Even though we do all we can to renew our minds, we never quite get there—perfection is beyond the reach of humanity—we are all a work in progress.

We are a perfect reflection of Jesus. In describing Him, we describe ourselves. His loving character, power and position—a perfect description of our character, power and position. Whatever is in Him is in us. He dwells in us in the person of His Holy Spirit.

Whatever we like about Him, we ought to like about ourselves. If there is not an ounce of shame in Him, then neither should there be an ounce of shame in us. If He is entirely righteous, then we are entirely righteous. If He is in right-standing with the Father, then we are in right-standing with the Father. If He is not condemned, then neither are we. If He is glorious, then so are we. The same love that is in Him is in us. We should not be asking if we are in right-standing with God; rather, we should be asking if Jesus is in right-standing with Him. If He is, so are we!

What is our personal worth to God? In order to know the value of an item, we need to know what the market is prepared to pay for it. What was the price paid for your ransom? Jews are very astute. No Jewish businessman worth his salt would ever pay a penny more than the true value of an item. Jesus, being a Jew, would not have paid a penny more for you than your true value. I am being light hearted here, but I trust that you are getting the point.

There is no getting around it—you cannot know your true value until you know what He was prepared to pay for you. How much did He pay? You cost Him His very own life's blood. Did you get that? If He is priceless, then so are you!

Is it possible that Jesus' value is not a penny more than your value? I don't know the answer to that question, but this I do know, God was willing to give Jesus in exchange for you. That being the case, it is obvious that you are intensely desirable to God.

In Jesus' prayer, as recorded in John 17:23, he stated that God the Father loves you every bit as much as He loves Jesus. Isn't this just the most marvellous news of all? The mere thought of it is intoxicating! God the Father does not love Jesus one iota more than He loves you! You must be very special to Him, even if you don't think so yourself.

In this scripture, Jesus did not mention any preconditions to obtaining this level of the Father's love. He didn't say He loves you for living right; He said He loves you, without making any mention of how rightly or wrongly you may be living.

Really? Does that mean that I am still loved when my behaviour doesn't come up to scratch? Thankfully, our personal performance doesn't even enter the equation. He is no respecter of persons—He loves all of us alike. He doesn't need us to give Him a reason to love us—He simply loves us because He wants to. End of story!

Our problem is not that we don't love Him enough. It's the other way around. Our problem is that we don't understand how much we are loved. A sense of shame messes with our minds—clouding our perception of His love for us.

We are not to renew our minds with our unworthiness. We are to renew our minds with His love for us. Although we will never fully comprehend the extent of it, the quest of discovering it is enormously edifying. Sadly, not all preachers understand the dispiriting dangers of harping on our inadequacies.

We need to visit God's mirror regularly to remind ourselves of our spotless perfection. Like a bodybuilder in a gym, we are to admire our good looks. Bodybuilders admire their strengths, not their weaknesses.

"*As He is so are we in this world*" (1John 4:17. NKJV). We are not trying to become like Jesus—we became like Him in a flash at re-birth. Although we were transformed in an instant, we need time to allow this transformation to work its way into our thinking so that it affects our day to day living in a positive way.

Not everybody benefits from the mirror. It all depends upon what we have been taught to look for in its reflection. Worthiness, or unworthiness; His power, or our weaknesses; His adequacies, or our inadequacies. Be sure to be wearing grace tinted spectacles.

Spreading the Word of Grace

Whenever I encountered misunderstandings among our friends concerning the fundamentals of grace, I would go to my PC and write them a simple explanation. These explanations became the nucleus of this book. My desire to see our friends liberated from the legalism that had kept me out of God's best, motived me to complete the project.

Before the addition of this chapter, I asked some pastors to read copies of the manuscript, and with bated breath, waited for their comments. I had no idea of how it would be received. To my surprise, they thought I was right on the money. Their encouragement reinforced my belief in the project.

All but my pastor had given their feedback, but with such overwhelming support, I felt sure that he would also get around to encouraging me. I eagerly anticipated his response. Eventually he phoned, asking me to visit him in his office.

To my dismay, he had concluded that my intention in writing the book was to slander him and his ministry. I was at a loss to understand how he could have come to such an unfortunate conclusion. Could I have touched a raw religious nerve? In my naivety, I did not know that the message of grace could be offensive to those who hold to the doctrine of mixing grace with law.

In subsequent private meetings with him, I did my best to convince him that he had misconstrued my enthusiasm for the goodness of God. My intention was to edify and uplift. Sadly, he refused to accept my explanation.

Over the next year, we met in private from time to time, but he remained vehemently opposed to my views on God's grace. After each private meeting, disheartened, I would take the matter up with the Lord in prayer, seeking His direction. Each time, God's instruction came through loud and clear—I was not to despair but to continue showing the pastor the love I had written about. Obediently, I promised not to take offence, but rather to show Him love, support and grace at every opportunity. Sadly, despite my best efforts, he remained firmly unconvinced.

After my last meeting with him and his wife, it was clear to me that I had hit a brick wall. Once again, my only recourse was prayer. This time God's answer was very different. He instructed me to walk away with love in my heart.

Although I had failed in my attempts to convince him of God's goodness, I trusted the Holy Spirit to continue encouraging where I had left off. Sometime later, I heard from his family that he had come to grasp these truths and was wholeheartedly running with the story of God's grace in a big way. Praise God for His faithfulness!

I have not included this story to shame this pastor. This church is no different to many other churches that have difficulty walking away from the comfort of performance-based holiness. To them, rigid restraints, frameworks and boundaries seem more dependable than the liberty afforded by grace. I have learnt that, from the safety of religious restraints, grace can seem awfully scary! Most believers do not take kindly to religious paradigm tampering. I understand this only too well, for I too made this transition with great difficulty—half a lifetime's contrary learning had to be undone.

At first, we may feel insecure at the thought of letting go—our Christian performance has given us a sense of security; albeit a false one. Paul did all he could to convince us that the law does not possess the power to make us right in God's sight. Despite this, much of the church continues to misuse law keeping to achieve worthiness—something that the law is incapable of doing.

It is difficult for leadership to switch from a message that mixes law with grace, to one that is purely grace. But if Paul was clear on anything, it was this—grace needs no help whatsoever from the law.

When we begin to understand how enthralled Jesus is with us, we become enthralled with Him, and before we realise what has happened, we find ourselves enthralled with right living. What more can the law contribute? Nothing but sin and death! Yes, we can measure our performances against the standard as set out in the law. No, we cannot make ourselves right by following it.

But in an environment of freedom and grace, leadership may fear losing control of congregants. Once the law has been abandoned for the sake of gaining the greater prize of grace, fear loses its right to control us—it can no longer be used to scare us into holiness—with grace, holiness comes naturally! Grace works with hearts; not with religious intimidation. Grace mixed with the tiniest quantity of Old Covenant law is not grace at all!

To this pastor's credit, long before I met him, he had already made some giant strides towards adopting grace. He was convinced that he had moved far enough, so he camped halfway. He was no longer practising the legalistic Pentecostal traditions and had dropped many lifestyle restrictions. He was sincerely convinced that he had discovered grace in all its fullness, yet he had not embraced its fundamentals, and without its fundamentals, what seemed like grace to him, was simply not grace at all.

Fundamentals to understanding the message of grace are:

- The unshakeable love of God that is in no way influenced by our personal performance, whether good or bad.
- The sinless identity of the believer. (We are the righteousness of God in Christ—established at rebirth, and remaining so for the rest of our days).
- Only love possess the power to change us from within.
- Power and authority were delegated to us at rebirth.
- Our behaviour, whether good or bad, has no bearing on the righteousness we obtained through the finished work of the cross—Christ did it all!
- Our inheritance is guaranteed by Covenant, without regard for our service to God.
- God continues to love and accept us exactly as we are, without demanding any promises from us.
- Outward piety, though commendable, does not impress God.
- We cannot truly change ourselves—it takes the love of God to do that.

Grace without its fundamentals is nothing more than legalism. When grace is compromised with legalism, grace is entirely cancelled. A miss is as good as a mile!

LEGALISM

Some may claim not to be living by Old Covenant law and therefore not to be legalistic. But there is more to legalism than that. Religious legalism is an obsession to conform to religiously devised piety in hope of obtaining God's approval. It presumes that God can be swayed by what we do or don't do.

We should ask ourselves whether this describes the relationship we have with God. If our answer is yes, we are plain and simply legalists—bewitched Christians with the same problem Paul encountered in the Galatian believers.

We are apt to describe good living Christians as spiritual. At funerals we often hear it said, "What a saintly man he was". But God has a different perspective on saintliness. The Bible tells us that His word is Spirit and that our good works are filthy rags. If the word of God is Spirit, then it follows that those who walk empowered by word and Spirit, are spiritual in His sight. In other words, people of faith! Those, who endeavour to be righteous, are not saintly; they are fleshly! From their pious demeanour, one would hardly think so. I must admit that, while I was under legalism's spooky spell, my perception of spirituality was precisely opposite.

Legalism is a symptom of a bigger problem. It is what believers turn to when they discover emptiness in religion. Religion is empty when it is no longer supernatural. Let's face it, legalism is nothing more than a poor forgery of the supernatural—clear indication of a less than healthy Father/child relationship. Although we are promised unlimited access into God's presence where prayers never go unanswered, many are caught up in the religious preoccupation of floundering for God's favour. Sadly, with legalism the miraculous is no more than a pipe dream; certainly not the norm!

Sure, we know that everybody receives the spirit of adoption at rebirth, but to be honest, how many of us actually enjoy intimacy with our Father, uncluttered by the thought that we may not have done enough to be in His good books? Unless we understand the liberating implication of being unconditionally loved, we will not be comfortable with divine intimacy.

Those who have been introduced to God the judge, will not experience the same intimacy as those who have been introduced to God the lover of their souls. Let's face it—it's difficult to be intimate with people who judge us, yet we have no problem welcoming lovers into the most guarded parts of our hearts. Thank God, there is One who has promised to look past our many failings.

Usually, the first generation in a fresh move of the Spirit experience this intimacy firsthand. Subsequent generations feel compelled to add caveats to romance—each generation adding more distance to intimacy. Before we know it, divine romance has been reduced to divine servanthood—Christian performance overshadowing divine intimacy.

Unfortunately, intimacy with the Father is not something that can be passed on to subsequent generations; it must be experienced firsthand. When we wake up to the fact that we are not experiencing the relationship and favour that was commonplace to our spiritual forefathers, we invent something else—substituting the supernatural with routines that mimic what was once supernatural. Sadly, it doesn't take too long for these routines to turn into religious rituals. That's when grace gets flushed out by legalism. But legalism is a far cry from intimacy—a poor substitute for relationship. According to legalism, I must do such and such to be worthy of intimacy, but according to grace, Jesus has done such and such to make me worthy of intimacy.

No matter how passionately we desire God's favour, it cannot be obtained through legalism's wonky idea of holiness. Previous generations did not obtain it by observing rules, they obtained it through first-handed relationship. What subsequent generations fail to recognise, is that the rules they construct to win God's favour, are the very rules that distance them from His favour!

Legalism does not bring us closer to God; it puts distance into romance. It substitutes the liberty and vibrancy of genuine affection, with the toil and drudgery of religion—a trade-off of divine warmth for nothing more than the dead works of religiousness.

We should ask ourselves: Have we slipped into the dreaded trap of trading our treasured divine relationships for nothing more than a list of powerless rules designed to make us look the part? Have we found comfort in religion? Have we slipped into ritualistic complacency? Have we settled for "doing stuff to appease God"? Ever wondered why our doings never seem to get us anywhere with Him?

Have we fallen for the fallacy that God would honour us for keeping humanly devised rules? Could it be that keeping these rules serve only to appease our consciences—giving us a sense of having done our bit for God? Have we been lulled into a false sense of security? In all of this, have we unintentionally shut God's best out of our lives?

Sadly, each subsequent generation experiences less intimacy, thus adding more rules to compensate for what they lack. But more rules serve only to put even more distance into God's favour. These rules eventually become church traditions. Just as you can tell the age of a tree by counting the concentric rings on its cross section, so you can tell the age of a particular denomination or church stream by the number of rules they observe. If we liken the pith of the tree to God, then each additional rule distances us a little further from the pith, putting ever more distance into divine romance.

Traditions don't have to be bad to be bad for us. They may even be good, but if we use them to find favour with God, they will stand between us and Him. Good things like reading the word, praying, fasting, church attendance, worshipping, witnessing and giving (all highly commendable), can be wasted if done simply because they are expected of us. None of these have the power to justify us—only the shedding of sinless blood can do that!

People are legalists, not because of what they do or don't do, but because of why they do or don't do them. Are they motivated by want-to's or by ought-to's and supposed-to's? The latter are legalists.

Legalism is a required compliance to a set of rules, and it includes compliance with the unrealistic expectations of church leadership. Even self-imposed ideals have a way of mutating into legalism.

Perfectionists are their own worst enemies, setting unrealistic standards for themselves. They are forever striving, but never quite good enough in their own estimations. When they fall short of their personal ideals, as they inevitably do, they turn on themselves, often beating themselves to a pulp. Extreme cases end up in psychiatric wards. They are compelled to be hard on themselves, repeatedly rehearsing thoughts of their failures and shortcomings to the point of self-condemnation and shame.

They cannot grant themselves worthiness, much less accept God's free grant of worthiness. They may be failing to be good at sport, business, parenting, relationships, weight watching, appearances, housekeeping etc. They never allow themselves the luxury of indulging in the joy of who they are. They forget that nobody is perfect.

They may wish they could retract words said in haste. Often spending days in regret for past indiscretions—damaging their self-images and trashing their self-worth. I have caught myself repeating the wards, "stupid, stupid", to myself while thumping my forehead. I have woken up in the middle of the night in a cold sweat with my mind racing through words carelessly spoken, not allowing myself the luxury of a peaceful night's sleep. In the perfectionist's opinion, every task could have been done better. Perfectionism saps every lost drop of pleasure out of the joy of living.

Perfectionists are not only dangerous to themselves; they are a danger to those around them. Having unrealistic expectations for their children, spouses, co-workers, pastors, fellow believers and friends. Relationships are often strained in the process. To them, doing a task properly is more important than relationships—high moral standards, more important than companionship.

Have we bought the lie that performance equals value? Fortunately, from our Father's perspective, we are valued without reason! He loves us every bit as much as He loves Jesus. He simply cannot add another molecule of love to a love that is already perfect. We are talking about divine love here folks! He is not impressed with piffling efforts at perfectionism. Our sincerest attempts at adding value to ourselves will get us nowhere—an exercise in futility!

The religious expectations that we impose upon our children do not connect them to God; they disconnect them from Him. All we achieve is to turn beautiful intimate divine relationships into dreaded religious chores. They will go along with our expectations while they have us looking over their shoulders, but discard them as soon as they fly the coop. Many pastors' kids rebel, not only against the high expectations placed upon them by legalistic parents, but against the very values their parents stood for. Doesn't that tell a story all of its own?

Those who live by less legalism, often point fingers at those who live by more—one legalist accusing another of legalism. But unless we have expelled every last vestige of legalism, we are plain and simply legalists. Whether we keep a little or a lot of law makes absolutely no difference, we are all in the same leaky boat. Even if we are only moderately legalistic, we are still nothing other than legalists! Even minute quantities of yeast in our lumps will ruin our loaves.

Legalism is ugly in any guise, harmful to self-esteem and diabolical to a divine romance. A poor substitute for a kingly reign with Jesus— a sure way to disinheritance!

Pride

Jesus could have paid compliments to a whole host of good people. Yet it wasn't the sinless, the strongest, the most faithful, His closest friends or most beloved disciples that earned His highest commendation. His choice took everybody by surprise.

He was the guest in the home of one of the most righteous of all men, yet it was not he who got a compliment from Jesus. Jesus was so complimentary of one individual that day that he said that as long as the gospel would be preached, her gracious gesture would be remembered.

The host of the house was wondering whether Jesus was for real. He felt that if He really was the Messiah, He would immediately recognise how pious and holy he was. A sorry quirk of the self-made righteous is that they expect to be admired for their piety.

The guests that day were drawn from the most respectable ranks of society. That is until an unexpected individual arrived without invitation. She was well known to them as a lady of the night, a whore from the rough side of town, though none of them would admit to knowing her.

She sat at Jesus' feet weeping, raining tears on His feet. Then undoing her long hair—something she had so often seductively done to lure weak men into her clutches, but this time, for a different purpose. She used her hair to mop up her tears from His feet, while smothering them in kisses. Next, she broke open an expensive perfume bottle and poured the contents over Him.

The host looked down his nose at her. In his eyes, Jesus was tainting himself with her shame. How dare she enter his righteous abode, and worse still, how dare Jesus accept a harlot's seductive routine. Then the thought came to him, "If Jesus was for real, He would be able to discern that this was a low bred filthy wench of no moral standing. If He really was who He had made Himself out to be, He would not be so familiar with filth. He would tell her where to get off before she contaminated the righteous atmosphere of the esteemed gathering". The fact that Jesus was fraternising with filth, only served to prove what he had suspected from the start. To His mind, "Such associations proved Him to be an impostor".

Jesus asked the host, "Two men owed money that they could not repay; one $50 000 and the other $5 000. The bank manager decided to write off the debts. Which of the two would be more grateful"? The host answered, "I suppose the one who was forgiven most". Jesus agreed with him.

Then he proceeded to say, *"Do you see this woman? I came to your home; you provided no water for my feet, but she rained tears on my feet and dried them with her hair. You gave me no greeting, but from the time I arrived she hasn't quit kissing my feet. You provided nothing for freshening up, but she has soothed my feet with perfume. Impressive, isn't it? She was forgiven many sins, and so she is very, very grateful. If the forgiveness is minimal, the gratitude is minimal".*

Then He spoke to her. "I forgive your sins".

That set the dinner guests talking behind His back: "Who does He think He is, forgiving sins"!

He ignored them and said to the woman, "Your faith has saved you. Go in peace" (Luke 7:43-50 The Message).

Overjoyed—genuine love was not something she had encountered in her line of business. The men who had used and abused her for personal gratification had destroyed her faith in the male species.

The host was not at all impressed—an extreme embarrassment to him, especially in front of the town's elite. His snobbery, a display of pride at its worst, was repulsive to Jesus, and for that matter, to sinners and saints alike. This kind of thinking comes from the self-satisfied egos of law keepers.

Pride is not at all pretty—it can go it alone and steal all the glory. Oh, how self-satisfying it is to be able to say, "I did it my way", like the signature song sung so arrogantly by Frank Sinatra. When we take the credit, we get the glory for our strength, wisdom and ability—enabling us to boast with smugness that we don't fall for what weak Christians fall for. How self-gratifying to have our devoutness noticed by people that matter.

When we choose to go it alone, we are saying no thank you to God's offer of grace. Pride is ugly in any guise—a by-product of legalism—it exalts us—we can say, "If I can be perfect, why can't you?"

Control is another by-product of legalism. If I can insist that you adopt my standards, I get to control you. I can say, "These are the rules I live by. If I can live by them, so can you". Religious control, righteous indignation, surreptitious manipulation, offence taking and pride are first cousins. Their surname is legalism. As a family, they do not understand the culture of mercy and grace that Jesus, Paul and the apostles so passionately proclaimed.

It is impossible for legalism and grace to coexist in the same person. The decision lies with each of us today: Will it be man's idea of religion, as defined by legalism, or God's idea of divine romance, as defined by His grace? Each of us is already in one camp or the other. A mixture will not do—half legalists are still legalists. Even the tiniest requirement added to grace, disqualifies grace altogether. *"For if you are trying to make yourself right with God by trying to keep the law, you have been cut off from Christ! You have fallen away from God's grace"* (Gal 5:4 NLT). We are either completely in grace or incomplete without it!

Self-righteousness is another by-product of legalism. Here's the deal—in my experience, it is easier to deal with self-righteous sinners than with self-righteous Christians. Self-righteous Christians are often quick to take offence—something that has got to be the least attractive attribute in a Christian—indisputable proof of un-grace. Conversely, graciousness is gloriously attractive!

A special connection takes place between strangers who accept each other exactly as they are without the slightest hint of judgement! There is an enchantment about grace—it is profoundly touching! Love has a way of getting to a person's soft side! True graciousness doesn't skip a beat when tested by ungraciousness—it simply refuses to take offence—choosing not to notice the faults of others.

Christians sometimes say that they are not judging others; they are merely judging their fruits. When boiled down to brass tacks, they are twisting Jesus' words: "You will know them by their fruits", to validate their criticism. But no-one has been commissioned by heaven's department of agriculture to be fruit inspectors. The "accuser of the brethren" is doing a thorough enough job of that all by himself.

Jesus had no harsh words for Peter for saying that he would not allow Jesus to be killed. Instead, He said, "Get thee behind me Satan". If you, like me, believed that these stern words were meant for Peter, you may also misperceive Jesus to be judgemental. No! Jesus wasn't addressing Peter with these words; He was addressing Satan. In the same way, we should immediately recognise who is behind the evil in our brothers, and have the grace to continue loving them without so much as a blink. If we are to hate sin yet love sinners, how much more should we hate Christian's sin yet love sinful Christians, warts and all?

The Armour of God

"Put on the whole armour of God, that ye may be able to stand against the wiles of the devil. For we wrestle not against flesh and blood, but against

principalities, against powers, against the rulers of the darkness of this world, against spiritual wickedness in high places. Wherefore take unto you the whole armour of God, that ye may be able to withstand in the evil day, and having done all, to stand. Stand therefore, having your loins girt about with truth, and having on the breastplate of righteousness; And your feet shod with the preparation of the gospel of peace; Above all, taking the shield of faith, wherewith ye shall be able to quench all the fiery darts of the wicked. And take the helmet of salvation, and the sword of the Spirit, which is the word of God: Praying always with all prayer and supplication in the Spirit, and watching thereunto with all perseverance and supplication for all saints" (Eph 6:11-18 KJV).

We are to put on the helmet of salvation and not the helmet of religion. The helmet of religion is our attempts to stay saved. The helmet of salvation does not represent our accomplishments; it represents God's. Let's face it, we could not save ourselves if we tried— our helmets consist entirely of Jesus' achievements and none of ours.

The difference between religion and authentic Christianity is that religion is man's attempts to reach God with good works, while Christianity is God reaching mankind with His good works. His good works were accomplished on Calvary. If we are wearing a helmet consisting of our efforts to be holy, our heads will have scant protection, exposed to Satan's onslaughts. Better that we don God's helmet of salvation. It's the finished work of the cross, and therefore impenetrable.

To state the obvious, salvation can only be accomplished by a Saviour. As exemplary as our behaviour might be; it does not add one iota to our salvation. Salvation stands purely on what the Saviour has achieved—any contribution we may offer cannot make it any more secure than it already is.

When we try to protect ourselves with "our" holiness, and not with Christ's, the enemy is not for one moment fooled. Why is salvation head armour and not chest armour? Our heads are where our understanding is located, and we are to renew our minds to all that our salvation encompasses. In other words, we are to understand who we are as regenerated beings in Christ.

It is inevitable, the righteousness we think we have achieved, breeds a sense of smugness. But our boast is at Christ's expenses! It does not draw us closer to Him; it distances us from Him.

When Satan sees the armour of God, he sees God and not the believer hidden within it. Once the visor on the helmet is clunked shut, Satan is confused. He remembers the time Jesus wore it—that's when Satan got his butt whipped. On that day, Satan thought he would be able to keep Jesus imprisoned, but little did he know, that would be the day he would be humiliated in the greatest defeat in history. Ever since, he has had a healthy respect for the armour of God.

Often, the armour of God is taught as our personal holiness. This cannot be right. If it were, it would be called the armour of the believer. Paul called it the armour of God because it consists of His salvation, His righteousness, His word, His truth and His good news! We are merely to put on the completed accomplishments of Christ.

After donning the armour, our part is to take on the enemy by standing our ground in faith—wielding the sword of the spirit—declaring God's word over every situation—incorporating prayer into everything we do. We are not left to take on the enemy in our own strength; we are to enforce his defeat by virtue of the finished work of the cross.

Before I came into this understanding, I was involved in a deliverance session. The demons just laughed at me, because at that time, I thought that my personal purity provided me with sufficient authority. Big mistake! The demons were not in the least bit intimidated. Needless to say, they stood their ground, and to my knowledge, never left the man.

If we are going to don the armour of our good works, we may as well lie down and play dead. Satan is not intimidated by flimsy armour. If we are hiding behind our holiness, we are exposed—vulnerable to his wily tactics. Thank God, we stand in the finished work of the cross—we are perfect in every sense of the word, and it is entirely Christ's doing!

Holiness

Holiness is often defined as the absence of sin. This is not what the Bible has in mind. Holiness means separate or different. God defined Himself as being holy long before the first sin was ever committed. That being the case, we cannot say that God was holy simply because he didn't sin. Of course we know that He is sinless, but that isn't the reason for His holiness. He is holy because He is separate and different. There is no God like Jehovah!

We are righteous, not because we do not sin, but because we were reborn into righteousness. We do not lose our righteous standing when we sin. If that was the case, everybody would lose their righteous standing seconds after rebirth—everybody sins—if not in deed then in thought. If righteousness could be obtained simply by the absence of sin, then we would be unrighteous in-between sinning and our next repentance. We would be yo-yo Christians, one minute holy and the next, unholy. This is the root problem with the teaching of "holiness by performance".

Righteousness is by grace alone. If it were not so, people would continuously be swinging back and forth, one minute righteous and the next unrighteous. Their righteousness regularly interrupted by judgementalism and the like.

For many Christians, holiness is a ding-dong battle—no sooner up than down—never quite sure whether or not their lives are right enough to obtain God's favour. How sad!

Christ has made us right with God our Father—we have become the righteousness of God in Christ. At no time do we stand in our own righteousness, we stand in someone else's righteousness. And it has nothing in the world to do with deserving it. Truth be told, we were not justified because we deserved it; we were justified because we did not deserve it! Imputed righteousness has given us indisputable right standing with God. We are now seated together with Jesus in heavenly places (Eph 2:6).

Our car's key does not fit the ignition of a friend's car, but if he gives us his key, we can drive his car. Similarly, our personal degree of righteousness does not fit the keyhole that unlocks God's favour. However, once He has given us His righteousness, we have His key to unlock it.

We are made new on the inside—not just sinners saved by grace—entirely new creations that never existed before—not even of the same species. We were of the species: "sinful man" before our conversion, now we are of the species: "righteous man"—we have been elevated to god-class beings—bearing our Father's DNA— *"As He* (Jesus) *is, so are we in this world"* (1 John 4:17b NKJV).

God no longer blames us for our sins; He blamed Jesus for them. Nor does He attribute our sins to us; He has already attributed them to Jesus. Since Christ has set us free from the law of sin and death, we are absolutely free, not two fifths or four fifths free. Not a single sin will ever be attributed to us for all time and eternity!

Now we relate to Him in terms of covenant alone. His Covenant grants us more favour than we could ever imagine—He calls it abundant life! When we add any performance to covenant, we get to feeling that we deserve to be rewarded, and when that happens, we lose access to covenant privileges.

New Covenant privileges are entirely free—they cannot be deserved—they can only be received through faith. To add good works, is to cancel covenant favour. *"And if by grace, then it is no longer of works; otherwise grace is no longer grace. But if it is of works, it is no longer grace"* (Rom 11:6 NKJV). Did you notice that the moment works are added to grace, grace is no longer grace?

Qualified without Perfection

Nothing that the New Covenant offers is cheap. It is so costly that nobody on the face of the planet can afford it. Thankfully, the price has already been paid in full—no further contribution is required of us. Access is not measured by our service; it is measured by Jesus' service. Christ qualified us all by Himself, without any help from us.

This usually bothers Christians who live righteous lifestyles by dedication, discipline and healthy habits. They are not impressed when undeserving believers are endowed with God's favour—they are likely to put it down to something other than grace.

For many years my quiet-time was a minimum of one hour per day and was often longer. If ever I missed an hour, I would make up for it by adding missed time to my next day's commitment. I would read through the Bible every year, and sometimes in six months. I would pray in the Spirit for a set length of time every day; I was on the church board; paid my tithes faithfully; gave generous offerings; sponsored Christian workers; was on the governing board of a para-church organisation; gave to missions; was a longstanding member of the worship team; was a house church leader; attended Bible courses; memorised Scripture; habitually confessed the word over sickness and poverty; cast out demons; prayed for the sick; witnessed to the lost; testified of His goodness and encouraged the down hearted. I thought that all of this qualified me for at least a little more favour than those who casually attended church. Yet as good as all of this was, I obtained no more of God's favour than the next man.

It is faith and faith alone that gets God's attention—it's the only means by which covenant promises can be unlocked. As far as righteousness is concerned, we are already fully qualified. The covenant is a done deal.

Paul had much more reason than most of us to boast. Yet He said, *"If anyone else thinks he may have confidence in the flesh, I more so ... But what things were gain to me, these I have counted loss for Christ ... and count them as rubbish, that I may gain Christ and be found in Him, not having my own righteousness, which is from the law, but that which is through faith in Christ, the righteousness which is from God by faith"* (Php 3:4-9).

Wow! As good as Paul was, he only counted on the righteousness he obtained through faith. And so it is for us! Anything else is plain and simply worthless *"rubbish"*!

THE GENTLE WAYS OF THE SPIRIT

I shared the goodness of our Lord with a technician while he was fitting a sound system to my car. He asked me if I would visit his home after working hours—he wanted me to help him and his girlfriend receive Jesus as saviour. They had been living together as a family for some time and had a one-year-old baby. They were doing their best to save enough money to get married, but were battling to do so on his meagre wage.

That night they joyfully accepted Jesus as their Lord and Saviour and embarked on an exciting new adventure in Christ. We met at church on the following Sunday. They joyfully responded to the altar call, wanting the whole world to know about the most wonderful thing that had happened to them. Unfortunately, their innocent enthusiasm was short lived—the joy of the moment soon quashed by Pharisee-ism. When the counsellor discovered that they were unmarried and living together, he told them that, now that they were Christians, they could no longer live together.

Seriously? Did he really think that God would want to destroy a happy family? Besides being economically impossible, this was not how the Holy Spirit would have handled this. Unfortunately, this was the last time they attended our church. The counsellor's attitude was typical of *"older brother"* mentality. This kind of attitude exists because the spirit of the Pharisee is alive and well in our churches. Pharisaic spirits can only operate where the law still exists. Somebody is keeping the law alive for his own devious purposes. You can guess who he is. It is part of his job description to *"steal, kill and destroy"*.

When the owner of a strip joint gave his life to the Lord in one of Bob Mumford's meetings, Bob was about to counsel him to close his sleazy business, but was prompted by the Holy Spirit to say nothing. This troubled Bob—he could not understand how a Christian could continue running a den of iniquity.

Some months later, Bob was overjoyed when the man returned to tell him that the Holy Spirit had been dealing with him. Bob naturally expected that the Spirit had told him to close his house of ill repute; only to be told that the Holy Spirit had directed him to stop watering down the whiskey! Seriously Lord? How could God allow one of His children to continue running a house of immorality?

Again, Bob wanted to jump in and tell him to close down, but once again the Spirit restrained him. Bob was most uncomfortable with this, but reluctantly went along with the Holy Spirit. It was only much later that the Spirit finally directed the man to close down. Bob said that he was glad he had obediently held his tongue. The Holy Spirit deals gently and with faultless wisdom and impeccable timing.

When the Holy Spirit guides us, though we have many sins, He chooses to deal gently, issue by issue; not overwhelming with everything all at once. Unfortunately, when the church rushes in to enforce holiness, the Holy Spirit often gets side-lined and the task gets bungled. But this is not the church's responsibility. The church is responsible for connecting new converts to the Holy Spirit. Once the connection has been made, the best the church can do is to step out of the way and let God be God.

When the church jumps in, overwhelming with rules and regulations, it succeeds only in impeding the Holy Spirit's gentle process of genuine sanctification. The church is commissioned to present the goodness of God and to encourage, edify, admonish and guide—it has no mandate to police God's children. Sometimes the church gets impatient with the Holy Spirit's progress and feels obliged to jump in and lay down the law. But when the church steps in with rules, the Holy Spirit has no option but to step out of the way.

A friend of mine gave his life to the Lord and immediately came into an incredible season of miracles. Almost every day he had a new story to tell me of wonderful miracles of healings, favour, and God's provisions. I had been serving God for many years and had not experienced nearly as many.

I am so grateful that God gave me the honour of introducing him to the basic principles of faith immediately after he was saved—a foundation that gave him a head start on his Christian journey. Fortunately, he didn't know anything less—to him miracles were supposed to happen—the supernatural was perfectly normal. Legalism had not been given a chance to subdue his childlike faith. By comparison, I had to admit that years of living up to legalism's demands, had left me content with a lesser Christian experience.

When he got saved, he was in a financial fix, not even having enough cash or credit to buy food for his family. No problem for him, he now had a heavenly Father who cared for him. In His mind, he was never going to want for anything again.

What was the outcome of his faith, you may ask? Food would be delivered to his doorstep from the most unlikely of sources. Without knowing of his predicament, both Christians and non-Christians alike would offload large quantities of quality food at his front door. He was eating better in his time of poverty than he had in times of plenty. He could hardly contain the delight of his new found faith—a glorious life, overflowing with abundance! Looking back, I am so grateful that

I had not introduced him to God the law giver. At first, he didn't know that god—He was in love with God, the lover of his soul.

But the church had other ideas. It didn't take too long for the church to convince him that it was unrealistic to expect to be blessed while there was un-conquered sin in his life. That's when he lost his innocence and became more aware of his sin and unworthiness than of His righteousness in Christ. Before long, he noticed that life was no longer miraculous. He lost his confidence and began to make excuses for not been able to live in God's provision.

The church had consigned a victorious overcomer to a life of mundane Christian drudgery. It seemed perfectly normal—other congregants seemed to be content with mundaneness. Although un-victorious, none of them would admit to it; they simply felt that what they were experiencing was all there was to Christianity. In reality, their faith had been impeded by feelings of unworthiness, the by-product of legalism. Their inability to keep laws and other rules doled out Sunday after Sunday, had caused them to tone down in faith, expect less and settle for unremarkable living. This church is not alone—many believers are routinely defrauded of their covenant rights.

A problem occurs when new converts are connected to clerical guardianship, instead of to Holy Spirit guardianship. Immediately after rebirth, new converts are given a string of well meant, yet profoundly disinheriting do's and don'ts. But despite the very best of intensions, these rules simply cannot be kept, making them more aware of their disqualification for sinfulness, than of their qualification through indisputable righteousness established by Christ. With a disinherited mind-set, there is little chance of embracing the victorious life that God had in mind for them.

Licence to Sin?

It never ceases to amaze me when Christians jump to the conclusion that grace equals licence to sin. I shouldn't be surprised. Paul had the same reaction from people when he taught grace. And he dealt with it in Romans 6:1-2. *"What shall we say then? Shall we continue in sin, that grace may abound? God forbid. How shall we, that are dead to sin, live any longer therein?"* (KJV). Sin is self-destructive—it is unconscionable to imagine that grace people would want to return to the very same self-destructive muck that they had been saved from.

"When God speaks of a new covenant, it means He has made the first one obsolete. It is now out of date and ready to be put aside." (Heb 8:3 NLT). In this verse, the relevance of the Old Covenant is settled once and for all. The Old Covenant is out of date, superseded, obsolete and cancelled in the lives of New Covenant believers.

Although we can be sure that the Old Covenant has been rendered obsolete, we can also be sure that the principles stated in it are not obsolete. If the covenant that forbade murder is obsolete, it doesn't follow that murder is okay under grace. Jesus made it clear when He said that our practical righteousness must exceed that of the Pharisees.

Pharisees lived strictly by Old Covenant Law. Under the Old Covenant, the actual act of murder was sin. But Jesus exposed this illusion. In His estimation, even unvented anger is as bad as murder, and lust, as bad as adultery.

As New Covenant believers, our positional righteousness is never in question. It was established once and for all time and eternity through the blood sacrifice of the New Covenant. Our day to day sin simply cannot cancel the righteousness that came to us through covenant. Seeing that this righteousness was not achieved by righteous living, it follows that it cannot be lost by unrighteous living. It is sustained by something far surer!

Obviously, this does not mean that our day to day sin should go by unchecked. God expects us to live by the principles of Jesus. But we do not do it in our own strength. *"For us to live is Christ"*. In other words, we have the privilege of allowing Him, who lives within us, to live His perfect righteousness through our day to day living.

Righteous living cannot be attained through any amount of striving; it can only be attained through obedience to the gentle leading of the Holy Spirit. Seeing that Jesus is within us, we have the privilege of living as He did. He continues His earthly ministry from within us— His actions and reactions becoming our actions and reactions. Problem solved!

Here is the burning question: "Who have we put in control of our choices: Our mentors, with their legalistic do's and don'ts, or the Holy Spirit?"

Living by the principles of the Old Covenant is not the problem. But a danger arises when we expect Old Covenant law keeping to be rewarded with New Covenant blessings. Let's settle this once and for all. The Old Covenant has been put aside—keeping its laws do not make us worthy of inheriting. The terms of the "Last Will and Testament" are clear and decisive—it has no codicils or addendums.

If you are thinking that, because of grace, a little sin won't harm you, think again! God may not have kept a record of it, but we still have to deal with the toxic fallout of our sin. Lying will cause others to distrust us, adultery will wreck our families and somebody else's, theft will put us in jail, greed will cause us to be avoided by all who know us, and unforgiveness will destroy our health and happiness, etc. None of these are fun outcomes. Let's face it—nothing that we get by compromising with sin is worth having.

Many make the mistake of thinking that, because the Old Covenant is obsolete, everything written in the books of the Old Testament is also obsolete. Moses' law only applied to 1500 years. That leaves 2500 years of Old Testament history that did not have this law to go by.

Other than law, the Old Testament is bursting with prophecy, faith, wisdom, love, patterns for victorious living, the favour of God, patterns for praise, worship and intimacy with God etc. All of this is every bit as important to New Covenant believers as the New Testament, and as such, should be cherished. The Old and the New both point to Christ. He is concealed in the Old; and gloriously revealed in the New.

Furthermore, the early church only had the Old Testament to go by. The New Testament had not yet been compiled—it came many generations later.

Even though Jesus' life was recorded in the books of the New Testament, He lived in Old Covenant times. It was not His birth that initiated the New Covenant; it was His death. The Old Covenant was not finished until, He declared, *"It is finished"*. He declared it while hanging on the cross.

The Old Covenant had full jurisdiction right up to the moment that Jesus exhaled His last breath. That's when the Temple curtain was torn asunder, marking the end of the Old, and the start of the New. At that precise moment, its laws were entirely fulfilled on our behalf, bringing about their immediate annulment! In voiding the covenant of law, its jurisdiction was eternally invalidated. It no longer has the power to bless or to curse. From then on, access to grace and favour would be through faith alone. *"He cancels the first covenant in order to establish the second"* (Heb 10:9b NLT).

In case you are still not convinced. Grace does not grant us a licence to sin—we already have one—we were born with it. We can go to hell if we want to. We can destroy our lives with sin—God allows us the choice. No! Grace is not a licence to sin; it is a licence to sanctification with the help of God's Spirit. It's a licence to escape from the failure of religious humanism, and from the law of sin and death.

This is such good news that it compels me to share it with as many people as possible—the very reason for scribing these pages.

My enthusiasm for God's goodness often gets me into a whole heap of trouble with religious folk. There are Pharisees out there ready to pounce on anyone daring to tell the truth of God's goodness. Beware! Pharisees are often found masquerading as God's anointed leaders. This is nothing new—Jesus was unpopular with the same group. I count it an honour to be vilified by religious people—as with Jesus and the apostles, I am in good company.

Liberty has a way of exposing what is hidden in our hearts. If a diligent law keeper abandons law in order to embrace grace, and then falls into lascivious living, then it is obvious that his years of law keeping had failed to change his heart. His new found grace cannot be blamed for what the law had failed to achieve in him. It may have restrained him, but it sure didn't transform him. And now that there are no restraints, his heart is exposed for what it is. Restraints do not infuse holiness into hearts; they serve only to drive un-holiness underground—hearts remain unchanged.

When the restraints are lifted, we are suddenly confronted with the real person. That's when law keeping is exposed for what it is— nothing more than a religious sham! If we are holy because we are restrained, then we are not in the least bit holy! We may feel obliged to project a perfect image, but that is not what holiness is!

The bottom line is that the law is powerless to sanctify. Besides, it was not instituted for that purpose. The law reveals sin; not righteousness. Yes, it exposes weaknesses; no, it cannot fix what it exposes!

Any counselling that requires a person to practice a set of religious rules to gain holiness is plain and simply godless counselling. Self-effort and self-change by their very nature are without god—far too superficial to provide a permanent solution—no more than humanism masquerading as religion. If we are not confident enough to leave sanctification in the hands of the Sanctifier, then we must admit that we do not trust Him sufficiently!

It should be obvious that our personal strength is too weak to overcome the enemy's strongholds within us. They are called strongholds for a reason—stronger than our best efforts. Thankfully, all power resides within us in the person of the Holy Spirit.

Paul advises us to renew our minds. That's where strongholds are situated. But the good news is that renewed minds are transformed minds with divinely inspired ideals. Problem solved! Of course, in reality, we do not always walk in unshakable faith. At such times, we are at liberty to seek the counsel and prayers of fellow believers.

When we are convinced of our authority, a certain confidence arises within. It takes nothing less than the authority of a believer to defeat strongholds; rules can't do it.

Isn't it amazing! Despite many years of counselling, the same people keep coming back to us with the same personal hang-ups. We shouldn't be surprised—rules do not work—they never have and never will! If our self-effort type counselling has failed to make the slightest difference, how then should we help people to attain lasting behavioural change? As usual, God's way is precisely opposite to ours. What is the antithesis of rules? It is grace and grace alone!

"Are you suggesting Deon that people should be told to just go on sinning because there is grace for them?" Not at all! I am suggesting precisely the opposite.

The only way for genuine change to take place in anybody's life is through the empowerment of God's grace. What they require is an understanding of just how much they are loved in their present less than perfect condition. Loved people behave differently—eager to yield to the One who loves them. Once the Spirit is given the reigns of their lives, the need for striving ceases! Problem solved!

How can we be sure that people will expose their hearts to the Holy Spirit? Again, God's word has the answer. We are to show them the goodness of God, because the goodness of God leads them to repentance (Rom 2:4).

Won't people abuse the goodness of God? Sometimes yes—it's the risk God has chosen to take. But when not abused, it results in repentance! What is His goodness? It is His unfailing love; kindness; favour; one-sided covenant; trustworthiness; faithfulness; mercy and grace. Besides getting to know His goodness towards us, we get to know our position in Christ. And that makes an enormous difference to the way we view everyday challenges.

We are the righteousness of God in Christ—seated together with Him in heavenly places; beloved children; highly esteemed; intensely desirable to our heavenly Father; the apple of His eye; co-heirs with Christ; blessed going in and blessed going out; blood washed; pure; spotless; brand new creatures that are incapable of being tainted by sin; irresistibly loveable to our Father; not having any of our sins imputed to us for all time and eternity (Rom 5:13).

When giving counsel, we can ask the person what the Holy Spirit is saying to them concerning their problem, then guide them to obey His voice and to do whatever He tells them to do".

The temptation to step in and help the Holy Spirit out by dishing out rules should be avoided at all costs. It could mean the difference between, "By our own might and power", which is neither mighty nor powerful, or "By His Spirit", which is the ultimate source of limitless might and power.

What is, "By might and by power"? It is "by self-effort", and we know that self-effort produces nothing other than *"filthy rags"* in God's sight. Obviously, the counsellor must be sensitive to the promptings of the Holy Spirit, ready to do as He directs. This is not meant to be a complete teaching on counselling, but rather a reminder to be cautious of dishing out rules.

Very often people are in a fix, not because of their own actions or the devil's, but because God wants them to come to the end of self-sufficiency, so that they can turn to Him for His all-sufficiency. Clearly, self-sufficiency would shut God's all-sufficiency out of their lives.

If we insist on going it alone, our personal achievements will give us something of which to boast. But our boast is at the expense of genuine change at the hands of the Holy Spirit. Our boast excludes Him from playing His life transforming role within us. But when we come to the point where we know that we only have weaknesses to boast of, God has opportunity to be strong on our behalf.

Self-sufficiency leads to smugness, which is nothing more than a product of pride. Pride leads us to judge those whose efforts are less successful than ours. Now instead of achieving holiness, we end up with two more sins, that of pride and judgement—our original sin times three.

Can we fall from Grace?

The answer is, yes we can! Do we fall from grace when we fall into sin? No—not at all! Sin does not cause us to fall "from" grace; it causes us to fall "into" grace. The Bible does not say, "Where more holiness abounds, more grace abounds"; it says, "Where more sin abounds, more grace abounds". Grace is not disqualified by sin; grace is intensified by sin! Granted specifically to defeat sin!

How then can we fall from grace? We fall from grace by merely attempting to make ourselves righteous through law keeping. *"Christ is become of no effect unto you, whosoever of you are justified by the law; ye are fallen from grace"* (Gal 5:4). Any amount of law added to grace disqualifies grace altogether. Any such endeavour is diabolical to our spiritual health and wellbeing—a practice to be avoided at all costs!

Are there any Hindrances to Receiving Grace?

Is grace conditional? Not in the least bit! However, we are given instructions to position ourselves to be in the right place at the right time to receive grace.

Is forgiveness a condition? No! When Jesus said that God forgives us to the degree that we forgive others, He was speaking to Old Covenant believers living under its laws—they did not have the benefit of the cross upon which all sin would once and for all time and eternity be dealt with. In Ephesians 4:32 Paul said, *"Forgive one another, just as God through Christ has forgiven you"* (NTL). Notice that Paul reversed the sequence. This seems like a contradiction until one accepts that Jesus lived in Old Testament times, while Paul lived under the New

Covenant of grace.

It was the cross that reversed the sequence. His death ushered in a very different covenant. Although we are forgiven before we forgive others; it does not make unforgiveness any more acceptable. People who bear unforgiveness and grudges are miserable, bitter and twisted and decidedly unpleasant to be around.

The problem with unforgiveness is that it is self-destructive and shameful. Also, our personal shame muddies our faith. Under the weight of shame, it is difficult to be emphatic in faith—there is always this nagging feeling at the back of our minds that our sins are getting in the way. Faith flounders in ifs and buts.

Unforgiveness is simply a symptom of un-grace. We cannot love more fully until we understand how fully we are loved. Scripture tells us that faith works by love—not our love—it's the other way around— faith works by knowing God's love for us. Trying to boost our faith by being more loving does nothing to boost our faith. Faith works with trust, and His gracious love gives us all the more reason to trust Him.

Isn't knowing God's Word a condition? No, but if we don't know His Word, how will we ever know what He has made available to us? Knowing God's Word grows our faith and exposes us to His love and wisdom—giving us all the more reason to trust Him. The more we renew our minds in His word, the more confident we become in prayer. "My *people are destroyed for lack of knowledge*" (Hosea 4:6 KJV).

Isn't prayer and fasting a condition? Prayer and fasting are vital to a healthy interaction with God. We walk in faith and authority to the degree that we know God, and we cannot know Him without dialoguing with Him. Prayer won't give us more of God's love, but it will help us to know how much we are loved.

Isn't holiness a condition? No. Our good works are as "*filthy rags*".

Jesus is our example—He gave people favour regardless of their law keeping—never once did He refuse to heal anyone. He never even told anyone to straighten out their lives before healing them. Seeing that Jesus required faith alone, how is it that we see a need to dish out religiously invented conditions. Jesus is so generous, so gracious—oh, what a wonderful Saviour!

Having said all of that, let's not kid ourselves—whilst everything is permissible, not everything is profitable; in fact misusing our liberty can get us into all sorts of trouble (1Cor 6:12). *"The eyes of the Lord watch over those who do right, and His ears are open to their prayers. But the Lord turns His face against those who do evil"* (1 Peter 3:12 NLT). These words do not contradict grace, but they do tell us how to position ourselves to receive what God freely gives. We should take Peter's words seriously; he walked in such power that even his shadow was potent enough to heal the sick.

Let's be perfectly honest, purposely doing evil is not walking in grace; it is misusing grace!

DOES GOD JUDGE US?

God is always the same, but not everybody understands this. Some see Him as gracious and unjudgemental towards sinners, yet judgemental and ungracious towards saints—as though schizophrenic.

How do we know that God does not judge us? He told us not to judge. Let's face it, He would never set a higher standard for us than for Himself. If He said that we are not to judge, it is because He wants us to be more like Him. He does not judge—judgement is something He has reserved for the end of the age.

Aren't trials and tribulations God's judgements? No! Difficult times are here for our welfare. Hard times build and shape our characters and faith—for our benefit; not our punishment—not signifying judgement; signifying love (Rom 5:3, 4).

God gave Adam dominion over the Earth and over everything in it. God did not give Satan any authority, dominion or power over the Earth. Satan lost all his authority when he was booted out of heaven, long before the account of creation in the book of Genesis.

If God didn't empower Satan, who did? Mankind in the person of Adam did it, and contemporary man continues to empower him. How do we do it? In the same way that we empower good outcomes, we empower bad outcomes. How do we empower good? By faith! How do we empower bad? By faith! Our words of doubt express unbelief, i.e. faith in reverse—a fear that our prayers may not be answered.

Couldn't God just step up and take back what Satan had stolen from us? Why couldn't he simply restore it back to us? Clearly, once a gift has been given, the donor forfeits control of it. If a recipient subsequently loses what was given to him, retrieving it remains the recipient's responsibility; not the donor's. Upon giving the gift, the donor forfeited all responsibility for it, and therefore has no right to interfere. Seeing man lost his gift of dominion, retrieving it was man's responsibility, not God's. Even if He wanted to, He could not violate His word—He is too holy for that! He had to come up with another solution.

This is His solution: He sent His Holy Spirit to Mary to conceive a God/man. The God/man, Jesus, went about this world establishing his identity as a man. Although He had every right to call himself the "son of God", he went about declaring that he was the "son of man". In calling Himself the "son of man", He was setting the stage to do for man what imperfect man could not do for himself; namely retrieve what man had lost to Satan. But to gain the legal right to do so, He had to be born of a woman.

He gave up His life of divine opulence and royalty to die on a cruel cross. Upon His death, the sin He carried, though none of His own, gave him entry into Satan's realm. When He entered Satan's territory, Satan thought he had foiled God's plan, but to his surprise, he was not able to keep Jesus imprisoned. Instead, the sinless "son of man" overpowered Satan and retrieved the keys of dominion from him. These were the very same keys that Satan had tricked Adam into handing over to him in the Garden of Eden.

Now Jesus offers the keys to any person who would want to be restored to full dominion. He does not force the keys upon anybody— He cannot—He had already given man a free will.

God does not interfere with man's independence and free will. We are free to do anything with our lives, even if it is shameful and harmful to us. God does not manipulate us; rather, he gently and lovingly spurs us on, using hard times and difficulties to help us back onto the pathway of blessing. God is altogether good. It is not in His nature to harm us, not even for our ultimate benefit. He offers to switch what Satan intends for our harm, into something to our advantage. We can either accept His kind offer, or sadly, allow a golden opportunity to slip through our fingers.

What about the shaking of God? Isn't that His judgement? No! He only shakes what is not of faith. The things that are good for us, like our right standing and kingdom privileges, cannot be shaken from us. His shaking is to rid us of all that is detrimental to our welfare.

We have a choice, either to stand in our own shaky self-made righteousness, or in the indisputable rock-solid righteousness of Christ—it cannot be a little of each.

When we really blow it big time, our self-confidence takes a dive. Nothing wrong with that! It may shake our self-assuredness, but that's an advantage; not a disadvantage. When all we are left with is Christ, we are left with infinite dependability!

Faith is the currency of the kingdom. As ambassadors of the kingdom, we are temporarily assigned to the kingdom's embassies on earth. Any embassy is sovereign and independent—not accountable to the laws of the country in which it is situated. The host country's laws do not apply to them; they live only by the laws of the country they represent. Ours is an embassy operating by the laws of faith within Satan's territory. As emissaries of the Kingdom, we don't operate by Satan's laws; we operate by the laws of the Kingdom we represent.

Although Satan would have us believe that our kingdom's currency is "works"; the monetary system and currency of the Kingdom of God is "faith" and "faith" alone! The "holiness" we manage to attain through good behaviour, should not be mistaken for Kingdom currency—good behaviour simply cannot be traded for favours. Satan does his level best to keep us from knowing this. Believers beware!

Once God has shaken off everything that is not of faith, we are left with brazen boldness—enabled to believe for more. Even if it does not make sense while we are experiencing the shaking, it will ultimately work out for our good. The part we play is to rejoice, and to expect matters to pan out in our favour.

The Bible says that Abel's blood cries out for revenge, but Jesus' blood cries out for mercy. Both were murdered, but the blood of each demands something different. Let's not beat about the bush—it was not Jesus' sins that got Him killed; it was ours. He has every right to cry out for revenge, but instead, cries out for mercy. Our sins did not bring about His wrath; they brought about His mercy!

This goes beyond the limits of earthly understanding—it speaks of the endless dimensions of His love for us. Does God judge us? No! He has already judged us, found us guilty and punished Jesus in our stead. God is too holy to punish two people for the same crime. His law of double jeopardy will not allow it—once we have been acquitted, we can never be retried for the same crime—our acquittal took place at spiritual rebirth. Jesus offered up His life for the sake of bringing mercy upon us, and His blood continues to cry out for mercy!

This is what Paul had to say on the subject of whether or not we are judged by God, "*Who dares to accuse us whom God has chosen for his own? Will God? No! He is the one who has given us right standing with himself. Who then will condemn us? Will Christ Jesus? No, for he is the one who died for us and was raised to life for us and is sitting in the place of highest honor next to God, pleading for us*" (Romans 8:33-34 NLT). I can't make it any clearer!

In case Paul is not convincing enough, what did Jesus have to say on the subject? *"The Father judges no one, but has entrusted all judgement to the Son"* (John 5:22 NIV). God our Father ceased to judge any of us when He gave Jesus the right to judge us. Then Jesus said, *"I pass judgement on no one"* (John 8:15 NIV). Jesus ceased to judge us when He stated that neither does He judge anyone. He reserves that right for the end of days. But even on that day, His blood bought children will not be judged for their sins. It's our works and motives that will stand or fall under His judgement. It is different for unbelievers—the unredeemed will be confronted with a terrifying prospect on judgement day.

As we look at the Pharisees of Jesus' time, we find that they were meticulous about religion to the degree that Jesus, the son of the living God, did not measure up to their "holy" standard. In their eyes, Jesus was grossly irreligious, irreverent and blasphemous.

Unfortunately, the spirit of the Pharisee is alive and well in our churches today. The sad thing about keeping rules is that it leads us, like the Pharisees, to compare ourselves with others.

A strange quirk of human nature is that we tend to look down on individuals who struggle with issues that we have managed to master. Don't forget that, no matter how many sins we have managed to master, there will always be other folk looking down their noses at us for different reasons. Judging others is ungracious, unbecoming, inappropriate and nothing other than an ugly symptom of gracelessness!

Could God be Unkind?

If no one in the history of mankind has ever managed to keep God's laws, then it would be grossly unfair of Him to hold out His favour as a carrot for keeping His laws. He knows full-well that nobody can keep them. If He were to do so, He would be putting His favour way out of reach. I am sure we don't need to be reminded—God, by nature, is incapable of unkindness. *"There is nothing but goodness in Him"* (Psa 92:15 NLT).

Satan aims to keep God's favour out of reach—he has a psychosis of keeping us at arm's length from our inheritances. Thankfully, we are not required to reach God through good works. It is He who reached us through good works—completing them on the cross!

Religion says, "Do, do, do". Grace says, "Done, done, done". Before Jesus died on the cross, He said that it is finished, and He really meant every word He said. What were we thinking? How could we even imagine becoming more righteous than God has already made us to be? Once God has finished doing something, it is complete in every sense of the word. Trying to help Him out with a little law keeping here and there, is not at all clever! And that goes for me too.

Much of the church has misrepresented the character of God for so long, that we have come to believe Him to be biased, favouring some and not others. But God is no respecter of persons. He made the same level of favour available to every believer at the precise instant of rebirth. But clearly, our personal experience of His favour differs. It all goes down to our paradigms—what we know and perceive of His character. His love assures us that our trust in Him is not misplaced. Unfortunately, if we chase after the wrong covenant, our faith will be compromised by a sense of unworthiness.

WHY DO WE NEED GOD'S FAVOUR?

God's favour? So what's the big deal? Millions survive without it! The answer to this question should be obvious. For as long as believers are not aware of their covenant rights, they cannot participate in them, thus allowing God's glorious favour to pass them by. Even though princes and princesses, they live as though they are street urchins begging for handouts from the King. The desperation in their prayers, a sure give-away—revealing what they know, or more correctly, what they do not know of their right-standing with God.

Are we worrisome beggars or dearly loved and cared for children? Is Christ a distant god or an indwelling presence? Without His favour, our every effort seems to be a senseless chore! It's like walking knee deep in mud—we seem to get nowhere fast. Is there a better way? *"Not by might nor by power but by my Spirit says the Lord of hosts"*. (Zec 4:6 KJV).

Why do airliners fly so high? If they were to fly any lower, they would encounter more resistance thus burning a lot more fuel. They need to break through into the jet-stream where the air is thinner, thus presenting less resistance to the journey. God has a far more effortless way for us to live. It is in the jet-stream of His Holy Spirit. With so much going for us, why would we settle for doing life the hard way? Sadly, many do! The choice is clear: Either we live in our limited strength, or in His limitless strength.

When comparing our strength to God's, on a scale of one to a million, how do we rate? One thousand? One hundred, or maybe ten? I would venture to guess that no man has ever reached one on the scale. The One who created the heavens and the Earth, and the fullness thereof, is immensely stronger than all of us put together. Seeing that He dwells within us, why would we attempt anything outside of His empowerment?

The choice is simple—we can choose to live by the weak arm of the flesh, or by the mighty power of the Spirit of God within us. Clearly, not a difficult choice!

What is Fullness of Life?

- Increase (growing into our destiny)
- Abundance (more than we can use)
- Joy (vivid emotion of pleasure—extreme gladness)
- Profit (excess of returns over outlay)
- Fulfilment (a sense of accomplishment)
- Blessed (endued with power to prosper)

"The thief cometh not, but for to steal, and to kill, and to destroy: I am come that they might have life, and that they might have it more abundantly" (John 10:10 KJV). God never intended for us to just barely scrape through. His intention is to endow us with "too much". Too much

joy; too much health; too much physical provisions; too much peace! Much more than we can possibly use on ourselves. He is the God of liberality and generosity; the God of excess; the God of super-abundance! He wants to bless us to the point of extravagance, so that our extravagance splashes over onto others!

Why We Need God's Power!

With His power:

- Our words are empowered to create
- Our prayers are empowered to be effective
- Our sowing is empowered to multiply
- Our witnessing is empowered to be effective
- Our work is empowered with favour and success
- Our spiritual insight is empowered to see more than the obvious
- Our understanding is empowered with wisdom
- We are enabled to create wealth in order to confirm the covenant of Abraham (Deut 8:18)

Compare our Options: It must be one way or the other; we can't have both. Choose well!

Grace plus Effort	Grace alone
• Saved by grace but work to stay saved.	• Saved by grace and kept saved by grace.
• Self-change—I must shape up and change the way I act.	• Divine change—not by might nor by power but by My Spirit says the Lord.
• Human betterment.	• Divine transformation.
• Strive for worthiness.	• Made worthy 2000 years ago.
• Restrained by the law.	• Led by the Spirit.
• Strive to modify behaviour.	• Loved hearts produce modified behaviour.
• Holiness through do's and don'ts.	• Holiness through changed hearts.
• Strive for God's favour.	• Rest in God's favour.
• Struggle with hang-ups.	• Rest in the finished work of the cross.
• Follow Old Testament law.	• Follow the law written on our hearts.
• Condemnation.	• Liberation.
• Guilt.	• Acquittal.
• Pride in self-achievement.	• Nothing to boast of—He did it all.
• Hope we have done enough to inherit.	• He has done enough for us to

inherit.

- Do, do, do.
- Done, done, done.
- Reminded of our sinlessness
- Reminded of our sinlessness in Christ
- Guilty—live in the shame of our failings.
- Acquitted—He took our shame upon Himself.
- Repent from sin and strive to stop sinning.
- Repent towards God who changes our appetite for sin.
- Ever striving to avoid the curses.
- Ever resting—Christ has redeemed us from the curses.
- The mirror reveals our sin and unworthiness.
- The mirror reveals our righteousness and worthiness.
- Submit to legalistic control
- Liberated from control.
- The church judges us—older brother mentality.
- Jesus defends us—He is our advocate.
- Strive to abstain from sin.
- Lose appetite for sin.
- Pharisaic attitude.
- Gracious attitude.
- Get nothing for striving.
- Get everything for believing.
- Easily offended.
- Takes no offence.
- Fruitless striving.
- Fruitful believing.

Clearly, there is absolutely no contest. The gospel of "grace plus lifestyle" simply cannot hold a candle to the gospel of "grace and grace" alone!

Facets of the Diamond

I was cautioned by a concerned pastor who felt that I had gone overboard on grace. He explained to me that grace is only one of the many facets of the diamond of Christian doctrine. Well, if that was true, then I was guilty as charged!

I had been on a mission to reveal God's goodness, unconditional love and mercy. Was I out of line?

It is true that Christianity is a multifaceted diamond with a myriad of wonderful doctrinal aspects. In accentuating one facet above another, I would be promoting an imbalanced Christian view—I had to agree with him! So, if grace is one of the facets, it should not be over emphasized—right?

How could I have made such an obvious blunder? But no sooner had I come to admit my error, than I sensed the Lord correcting this perspective. Here is His perspective on this issue: Grace is not one of the facets of Christian doctrine. All other doctrines are facets. If grace isn't one of the facets, then where does it feature?

When I got God's perspective on this, it blew me away! The reason that grace is not a facet is because grace is the whole diamond of Christianity. Grace itself has many facets—each a cherished Christian doctrine. And God expresses His love to us through each facet of His grace. Name any facet of Christian doctrine: healing, prosperity, love, peace, joy, faith, hope, kindness, mercy, redemption, holiness, righteousness, deliverance, service to humanity etc. All are facets— each adding to the sparkle of the diamond. The whole diamond is grace!

We can't have any of the above, except through His grace. Grace is not an optional extra—it is everything—the very essence of

Christianity! It's the core of everything that pertains to believers' entire Christian walk. Other than grace, there is nothing in it for believers. Let's not pussy foot about this point—without grace Christianity does not even exist!

Consider healing as an example. Is it by our power, or by His that we are healed? Well, His of course! Therefore, healing is of grace. The same can be said of every other aspect of our Christian walk. Whatever we can achieve without God's help is not by His grace. Clearly, anything and everything desired of Him, can only be obtained by faith through grace.

How often have we bumped our heads trying to do things our way? We could have avoided these unfortunate bumps if we had effortlessly surfed in on the waves of God's grace and favour. Seeing that His empowerment to walk in victory is always available to us through grace, why on earth would we settle for anything less?

To understand grace is to understand God's perfect love. If we were to presume that God is not gracious, why would we even bother with prayer? We'll get more value out of a game of tiddlywinks. It is grace that gives faith a reason to be confident—without grace, prayer is pointless!

There is no point in believing for anything from God, unless we are assured that our sins are not getting in the way. It should be obvious that no-one is ever going to attain perfection in practical terms. That being the case, for God to bless us, He would have to find a reason to look past our many sins and failings. Thankfully, He has provided such a reason—it's by way of the blood of His Son—unquestionable proof of His mercy and grace. Seeing that He went to such enormous lengths to reach our hearts, it would be safe to imagine Him attending to lesser matters such as blessing our daily living?

If we settle for the facets of doctrine, while missing the truth that they are merely facets of something far bigger, being God's loving grace, we end up with empty doctrines lacking divine power! Clearly, we have no access to any of the many facets of Christian doctrines other than through His mercy and grace. I cannot make this point strongly enough—all the many facets of Christian doctrines are merely extensions of His grace.

Take grace out of Christian doctrines, and we end up with nothing more than Islam or one of the other self-effort religions of the world.

"Yes, we know grace is important", you may be saying, "but we need to balance it". Sounds perfectly reasonable, doesn't it? But when it comes to grace, balance presents a dilemma! What could possibly be used to bring balance to grace? There is only one commodity, and tragically, that is law!

Well, what so wrong with law? When discussing law, Paul warned us to beware of the leaven that leads to a yoke of bondage. He warned us that, in balancing grace with law, we would fall from grace (Gal 5). Beware! Even to add one tiny law to grace, would cancel all that grace is. Zero grace equals zero favour, and a barrier that separates, instead of a divine romance that blends us with divinity. Either we live by law or by grace. It has to be one or the other. I trust you have made the right choice!

Before Jesus ushered in grace, the scales were seriously out of balance—certainly not tipped in our favour. The law condemned us, and this prevented us from participating in God's favour. God solved this dilemma, not by finding a balance between the two concepts, but by overwhelmingly outweighing law with mercy and grace. In finding a balance, we would still have some law to fulfil—enough to curse us and keep us out of our inheritances. No! God completely outweighed the law. We can balance any other aspect of our lives, but we dare not balance grace! We cannot afford to invoke the law's many curses! In doing so, we would be trading our God given freedom for bondage to works of the flesh!

With the law, I can take credit for my successes, because it is all about me and what I have achieved. But with grace, all the glory goes to Jesus alone—He achieved it all by Himself! With the law I receive curses for my failures, but with grace I receive mercy for my failures. Not something that can be balanced! It has to be all or nothing at all! By its very nature, grace does not even exist when balanced against the tiniest molecule of law!

Clearly, it must be one or the other—we can't have it both ways. I trust that you have chosen well! Thankfully, it is by no means a difficult choice!

Who does What?

In any enterprise it is important for all parties involved to be given precise job descriptions. This helps individuals focus on what is expected of them, and to ensure that there are no unnecessary duplications of tasks. In a manufacturing business, it is important for the floor sweeper not to do the books, or for the storeman to not construct products.

What then is our job description in the matter of sanctification? It is to accept that God loves us in our less than perfect state, and does not expect any promises from us to change.

Doesn't His love just make the thought of surrendering appealing? It is not at all difficult to yield to someone who loves us so unconditionally. What about untamed behaviour? No problem there—sanctified behaviour soon follows as a natural consequence of being overwhelmed with God's affection as expressed in His grace.

Doesn't our job description include changing the way we behave? No! Is it God's job then? No again! Our behaviour is not what needs changing. Our behaviour is simply the outworking of what's in our hearts. While our hearts are being transformed by His love, our behaviour needs absolutely no modification. Our behaviour simply follows the attitudes embedded in our hearts by love. Purified hearts produce purified behaviour.

Why doesn't He just automatically change our hearts when we get born-again? He is too holy to interfere with our right to choose. He relates to His children; not to His puppets—puppets do what the puppeteer makes them do. Unless we have a right to choose, He cannot know whether He is truly loved. For worship to have any meaning, it must be given willingly.

Heart change is not a onetime experience that magically makes us perfect; it is a whole lifetime of many small adjustments called sanctification, and nobody lives long enough to complete the process. In a practical sense, although moving in that direction, nobody reaches perfection this side of eternity.

Simply put: Divinely changed hearts make better choices. Without God's open-heart surgery, our choices are often self-destructive. Unloved hearts are apt to make poor choices.

It wasn't our minds and bodies that were transformed at rebirth; it was our spirits! Our bodies need to be offered up as living sacrifices, and our minds need to be continuously renewed (Rom 12:1,2).

We can rest assured; our righteous standing cannot be nullified by our sins. It is important to continuously remind ourselves that we are every bit like Jesus. All the beauty embodied in Him, is embodied in us!

When the Bible refers to our hearts, it is referring to that mysterious part of our beings called the subconscious mind. Within it, rigid paradigms are formed by a lifetime of personal experiences that have shaped our unique world views. Nobody has access to their subconscious minds and thus are powerless to change the way intuitive thinking takes place. The sum-total of all our past experiences, whether good or bad, have predetermined the way we act and react, in much the same way as a computer programme predetermines the way a computer processes information.

In that case, does it follow that we will not be held accountable for our actions—after all, our subconscious minds are beyond our reach? No! We most certainly will be held accountable. But we are not left without help. The Holy Spirit is willing and ready to come to our aid.

Isn't there punishment for sin? Yes! But fortunately, the punishment due to us was not charged to our accounts; it was charged to Jesus' account! We know this because, *"God was in Christ, reconciling the world to Himself, no longer counting people's sins against them"* (2Co 5:19 NLT). But there will be many who will have to face the terror coming their way, not for their sins, but for not accepting redemption (Joh 16:19).

That does mean that there are no consequences for sinning saints. The natural consequences of sin are not at all pretty. Sin is like eating a prickly pear without pealing it—it's microscopic thorns will get you. God will give us many opportunities over the rest of our lives to co-operate with His Holy Spirit in a continuous process of heart changes.

Just being loved when we don't deserve it is immensely heart captivating—the most influential force for social change known to mankind! Prison time can't change hearts for the better, and religious pressure is equally ineffective. Religious moral codes are powerless, except to disinherit saints. Only love can change hearts for the better!

God does not expect us to pull ourselves together; He loves us in our less than perfect condition. Just knowing this is enough to melt our instinctive resistance to change. Something as self-destructive as sin simply cannot compete with the edification of being so completely loved. Unconditional love is irresistible—sin's allurements simply cannot compete with divine affection—temptations soon lose their shine!

God does not overwhelm us with a list of defects to be fixed. No, He works gently, at a pace that we can manage. It is not a quick fix; it's a lifelong process!

Very often, we may be amazed at the favour He shows to people that, to our minds, don't deserve it. Ever wondered why longstanding Christians often enjoy less favour than new converts? New converts are still enjoying their new found forgiveness, freedom and innocence. They have not been waylaid by Religion's many rules. But sadly, not so for many longstanding believers who have been robbed of their innocence by religious guilt and condemnation. When one is bombarded with messages on sin, rather than righteousness, what more can one expect!

Instead of the church allowing the Holy Spirit to deal with us little by little, it rushes in to fix everything all at once. Is there any wonder that we acquire a sense of shame and unworthiness? No wonder our prayers are often plagued with faith destroying doubts—keeping our inheritances out of reach!

Our Eighth Day Experience

What role does baptism play in heart change? Until recently, I had understood that baptism was an act of obedience, symbolising our death and resurrection together with Christ. This seems to be the general teaching on this subject by denominations practicing believer's baptism. This understanding is not wrong, but it is only one aspect of what happens at baptism. If this was all that there was to it, then we would have to admit that baptism is merely a religious ritual. But the New Covenant is not a covenant of rituals; actions lead to divine outcomes.

Jesus was wounded for our transgressions and bruised for our iniquities. There are transgressions and there are iniquities. They are definitely not one and the same thing—God does not put words on a page simply to take up space—He carefully chose every word for a specific reason. A transgression is an act of transgressing the law; while an iniquity is an elusive weakness beyond our control.

We may have given it our best shot, but like a bothersome fly, our iniquities continue to bug us. Eventually, in sheer exasperation, we resign ourselves to put up with them. Very often these iniquities are passed down through bloodlines as generational curses and can take on many forms. Some iniquities manifest in bad habits and antisocial behaviour, while others, in illnesses and diseases. Bad habits are not necessarily confined to the obvious ones, such as smoking, alcoholism, pornography and drug taking. It could be a critical spirit, unforgiveness, offence taking, ungraciousness etc. Anything that is beyond our ability to master.

Paul explained that we are circumcised by baptism, in the same way that Jews were circumcised on the eighth day (Colossians 2:11, 12 amp). Most Christians do not understand that our baptism is the act of cutting away the flesh. It is our eighth day experience.

Most Christians, including myself, missed the significance of this most vital aspect at the time of our baptisms, and this has left us with incomplete baptisms. I am not advocating more than one baptism; however, I am advocating completing the first one if it is incomplete. We may need to go back to the water to have our fleshly iniquities cut away by baptismal circumcision. Drawing up a list could help identify exactly what iniquities we want cut away at baptism. I did, and my list was surprisingly long. This step may be key to victory over offensive behaviour and undesirable habits.

Circumcision of fleshly iniquities does not guarantee that we will not have to deal with the same issues in future, but it does empower us to make better choices. Without this cutting away, we are often left powerless to deal with stubborn iniquities—it is as though we are driven by them. It is not unusual to be surprised by one's own caustic reactions. Have you ever found yourself wondering where those impulsive hurtful retorts came from? They are still lurking in our hearts. Though we spend a lifetime trying, we just don't seem to be able to shake them. But in baptism they can be circumcised.

"Out of the abundance of the heart the mouth speaks". We are not able to have victory over our mouths until we have victory over our hearts—reprogramming is needed. God's unconditional love has the power to do it!

COVENANT

Adam's Self-Effort

Adam and Eve failed to stand in their own righteousness. After falling for Satan's trickery, a sense of guilt set in—something they had never experienced before! After having lost their innocence, they felt ashamed for being naked. In their embarrassment, they did their best to conceal their shame, clothing themselves with leaves. But their very best attempts did nothing to remove their sense of shame. They needed help—they needed God, but their shame had gotten in the way! Seeing their plight, God decided to give them a lesson they would never forget. It would take nothing less than innocent blood to rescue them from their embarrassment.

Fortunately, long before Adam's fall, God had already decided on a plan of action to rescue him and his descendants. Although God requires justice to be served, He had no desire to punish Adam or his descendants. However, a just God cannot allow injustice to go unreconciled. Someone would have to pay for Adam and Eve's blunder. Fortunately, God's mercy exceeds His justice. He decided on

131

substitutionary punishment. But for the task, He required the blood of a perfect man—one who is not already condemned for His own sins. Of course, we all know that such a person has never existed. Being imperfect, mankind could only offer up imperfect blood, contaminated with humanity's many imperfections.

So, in His love for mankind, He sent His Son to be sacrificed for mankind's sinfulness. But for this, He had to have a body of flesh and blood. So, to legitimise His humanity, He had to be born of a woman. Only then did He qualify to be sacrificed for humanity.

Once qualified, Jesus purposely laid down His life for us upon the cross. It was here that an exchange took place—His righteousness exchanged for our unrighteousness. Now, despite our sins, we stand blameless without a single dot of unrighteousness to blemish our right-standing with God.

How could this help Adam and Eve who lived four thousand years before Jesus? God had to use the blood of something totally innocent to stand in for the blood of Jesus, until such time as Jesus could shed His blood for them. So, He sacrificed an animal in order to clothe them, thus giving them the righteousness belonging to that innocent being.

So often, we do our best to modify our behaviour, thinking that it will make us worthy to inherit. As with Adam's leaves, our self-effort cannot do it. It doesn't give us access to God's favour, nor to our inheritances—for that it takes faith from our side and grace from God's side!

We are highly favoured, not by reason of what we have or have not done, but by reason of a testamentary bequest naming us as beneficiaries. We are not required to prove ourselves by reaching a certain level of holiness. Anybody who has been around the block a few times, knows that all believers fall short of the glory of God.

Covenant

We do not covenant with God. Christ has already done it on mankind's behalf. There is nothing more for us to do except to make testamentary withdrawals. Jesus' humanity gave Him the right to make covenant with the Father on humanity's behalf. Covenant was cut on the cross and sealed with the blood of Jesus.

In any covenant, the stronger party to the covenant is obligated to stand in for the weaker. Our responsibility to the Covenant is to acknowledge our weaknesses; God's responsibility to the Covenant is to make up for our weaknesses with His strengths. Thus, we are able to count our weaknesses as strengths—they are made perfect in His strength (2Cor12:9).

God has bound Himself to an eternally irreversible Covenant—the strongest form of vow! Why would anyone want to live by their own ability to gain health and other provisions, when they could just as easily be living by His health and provisions? He has given us free access to health for our sickness, wealth for our poverty, wisdom for our foolishness, joy for our sadness, peace for our chaos and so much more.

David made a covenant with his friend Jonathan in terms of which everything owned by either party, would be available to the other. This covenant extended to the wellbeing of each other's families.

After Jonathan and his family died in battle, David became King. To his knowledge, none of Jonathan's family had survived. It was only very much later that David discovered that Mephibosheth, Jonathan's son, had survived. He immediately sent for him, to restore to him his rightful share of everything he, David, owned. As King of Israel, David's wealth afforded him an extremely lavish lifestyle. Mephibosheth, on the other hand, had lost everything and was living in dire poverty. He had no idea that King David would honour a covenant made so long ago with his late father. He had accepted dearth and squalor as his lot in life—resigned to eke out a pitiful existence on handouts.

When Mephibosheth came before the King, his self-esteem was so low that he found it difficult to accept anything from the King. His words revealed how little he thought of himself, referring to himself as a "dead dog".

David declared that he would take care of Mephibosheth with real estate and royal favour. In view of Mephibosheth's disability, Ziba was assigned to act as his guardian. Sadly, his trusted guardian cheated him out of his newly acquired wealth. When David heard about this travesty, he decided to restore half of what Mephibosheth had lost to Ziba's embezzlement. But Mephibosheth was so low on self-esteem that he turned David's generous offer down (2 Sam 9:1-13 & 19:24-30).

Like David and Jonathan, God made a Covenant with us in terms of which we are co-owners of all of Jesus' wealth. We, like Mephibosheth, were living in squalor, when we could have been living as sumptuously as kings. But for as long as we were not aware of our covenant rights, we continued to live in lack.

Unfortunately, even though we came to know what we were entitled to, in terms of God's Covenant, our shaky and ineffective attempts at law keeping kept us in a state of unworthiness. So, we let God's kind offer pass us by. Much like Mephibosheth, we just didn't feel deserving enough to boldly step out and receive our share of God's countless treasures. Worse still, religion congratulated us for our humility.

Nobody seemed to notice that this was Satan's ploy. He sets us up—gets us to strive to keep the law as a means to make ourselves worthy of God's favour. He knows we'll never achieve our objective—no-one has! Yet we strove on regardless, stumbling along a pathway to nowhere—each transgression making us feel ever more unworthy. Eventually, like Mephibosheth, we felt so worthless that we ceased to expect anything at all. And so, our inheritances slipped through our fingers.

Though rightfully ours, we settled for less. It took nothing more than the legalism imposed upon us by our trusted spiritual guardians to disinherit us! When we look to the law for our right-standing, our weaknesses loom large in our minds, ensuring that we don't reach the point where we feel worthy of claiming what is rightfully ours in terms of the Covenant.

Beware! Even if we do receive our Covenant rights, Satan is not going lie down and play dead. Satan is our Ziba, seeking any opportunity to cheat us out of God's favour. Eventually, Ziba was allowed to keep what he had stolen from Mephibosheth. In the same way, Satan robs us, and then, because of groundless feelings of unworthiness, we cease to fight back. Satan takes advantage of our dispiritedness, as if invited to deprive us of our property.

If it had been left up to us to make covenant with God, we would most likely have compromised it with a sense of unworthiness, and that's why Jesus stepped in and did it for us without any help from us.

He cut Covenant with His Father on mankind's behalf. Thus God effectively cut mankind's Covenant with Himself, making it flawless from both sides—eliminating any and all human fallibility from the equation!

After Covenant making, Jesus bequeathed all Covenant rights to us in terms of His "Last Will and Testament". Of one thing we can be certain—His endowment of favour is doubly secure—not only in terms of unequivocal Covenant, but also in terms of a gratuitous bequest!

We do not have to wait until we are worthy enough to receive God's favour—nobody is! Although the bequest is already legally ours, we get none of it, unless we use faith to appropriate it. We are quite at liberty to do so whenever required. Mankind's covenant rights are freely at our disposal—we are at liberty to deal with them as we see fit.

Unless we grasp the fact that our ownership rights were established by Divine Covenant, we are unlikely to understand grace correctly. Perspectives are likely to be distorted by the notion that it must be deserved. But Covenant assures us that whatever we require in life has already been granted in advance—not appropriated according to worthiness; appropriated according to faith! To be perfectly frank: Other than through Covenant, we have absolutely no connection to God!

There was a man who saved up for many years to go on an ocean cruise. He eventually accumulated sufficient to purchase the fare. The cruise was great fun, except at meal times. When everybody else would be served lavish dinners in the palatial dining room, he would dash down to the cramped confines of his little cabin to eat stale sandwiches from his picnic basket. You see, he had only saved up enough money for the fare and could not afford the meals.

At the end of the cruise, his fellow passengers asked him where he had disappeared to at mealtimes. He reluctantly admitted that he could not afford the meals. His answer astounded them—the meals were included in the price of the fare.

Sumptuous five course meals were waiting for him every day—he just failed to pitch up for them. He lost his privileges purely because of ignorance.

If we do not know what our covenant rights are, we too will fail to appropriate them, and consequently forfeit them (Hos 4:6).

Many wonderful Christians live their entire lives without using any of their blood bought Covenant privileges—content to eat the stale sandwiches of dead religion. They live underprivileged despite being invited by the palace to dine extravagantly with their Divine Father at the King's table. They may even feel that they are being humble and saintly by living in lack. But nothing could be further from the truth.

Clearly, refusing God's Covenant is not a sign of humility. Humility is the act of humbling ourselves under God's will. His will is that we should enjoy our Covenant rights. Afterall, He obtained them for us at great personal expense.

There can be no greater insult to Jesus than to shun His kindness. Refusing a gift is not the best way to honour anybody, let alone Jesus, especially considering the lengths He went to—the enormous price He paid. If true humility is laying down our pride before his will, then humility equals abundance, not lack.

Did the Law nullify Abraham's Covenant?

"This is what I am trying to say: The agreement God made with Abraham could not be canceled 430 years later when God gave the law to Moses." (Gal 3: 17 NLT)

Abraham's Covenant is also our covenant—Jesus ensured our inclusion. It was a Covenant made between Abraham and God without any preconditions to fulfilling law—there was no law at that time. In fact, there would be absolutely no law for another 430 years. It took that long before the law was eventually introduced by Moses. The blessings of Abraham's Covenant were free and unencumbered by any legalistic requirements. 430 Years later, Old Covenant Law was brought about, lasting for a period in history.

Then came Jesus! On the cross he fulfilled all the requirements of the law; bringing its jurisdiction to a decisive and final end! But God's Covenant with Abraham remained unconditional right through the law's existence, and continues to apply to us without conditions. It began without Abraham having to fulfil any law, and continues to benefit us, without us having to fulfil any law. We share its benefits in the same way that Abraham did—by faith, without a single law!

Just like Jesus' Covenant of grace, Abraham's Covenant was also one-sided. God put Abraham to sleep while making covenant with him, so that he would not invalidate it with words of doubt and unbelief.

Later, because Abram would most likely have talked himself out of its promises with words of doubt and unbelief, God had to rescue the situation. God had promised him a son, but in reality, pregnancy was highly improbable—His wife was way beyond child bearing age.

It was obvious that Abram was having difficulty declaring that he would become a father of many nations. God does not control our words or our faith, and therefore could not force him to be a father—freedom to choose remains in the hands of mankind. If there was going to be a miracle, it would have to be declared into existence by Abram; not God.

To get around this obstacle, God had to come up with something that would cause Abram to declare His faith. And He did it by changing the pattern of his speech. To accomplish this, He changed his name from Abram to Abraham, meaning "father of many nations". Now every time he introduced himself to anyone, He would have to declare, "Pleased to meet you. I am the father of many nations". Even though this was far from reality, he would be speaking "creatively", thus declaring the promise into existence—speaking of those things which were not reality, as if they were.

Speaking things into being was the way that God created everything that can be seen. Before He said, "Let there be light", it was dark. When He spoke these words, His words took on physicality, manifesting light. He expects us to imitate Him—we have been granted the power to use our faith to create—we do it by declaring things into existence by faith in Jesus' name!

Abraham had full access to the benefits of the covenant by faith without any help from law keeping. And it is precisely the same for us!

Purpose of the Law

Does Old Testament law have any relevance in our day and age of grace? Certainly! It's the schoolmaster to the sinner.

Firstly, it reveals God's perfect standard. If we insist on standing in our own righteousness, then nothing less than perfection would be required of us. In fact, we would have to be as perfect as God. The law demands absolute faultlessness—anything less is worthy of a curse. One thing is certain—God did not compromise His Covenants with escape clauses. If we are guilty, then we are guilty, and that settles it!

Secondly, it shows us our sinfulness, and just how far short we are from His glory.

Thirdly, we soon realise that it's standard of perfection is not achievable—God's standard is simply too high for mortals. We are incapable of truly changing ourselves—no-one has ever succeeded in keeping all the law.

Fourthly, it shows us our desperate need of a saviour!

Although the law shows us our sin, it is incapable of putting us in right standing with God. For that we must look beyond the law—it's got to be by some means other than our flawed efforts to make ourselves right. For that, we need a Saviour, because without one we are seriously without hope!

Jesus said that He had not come to destroy the law, but to fulfil it. Notice that He said that it is He who would fulfil it—not us. He would do it on our behalf, so that we would not have to do it for ourselves. Now that He has completed the work of perfecting us for all time and eternity, we are cautioned to leave the law alone. The law is not for New Covenant believers, it's for unbelievers—it's their schoolmaster, revealing their desperate plight without a saviour.

Guardianship of the Law

"Think of it this way. If a father dies and leaves great wealth for his young children, those children are not much better off than slaves until they grow up, even though they actually own everything their father had. They have to obey their guardians until they reach whatever age their father set. And that's the way it was with us before Christ came. We were slaves to the spiritual powers of this world" (Galatians 4:1-3 NLT). This scripture is not intended to

put new Christians under the guardianship of the law. Guardianship applies to unbelievers only.

Very often the reason that new Christians do not live victoriously, is because they are robbed of grace by well-meaning legalists who insist that, despite grace, they are still under the guardianship of the law. Sadly, for as long as they must give answer to the law; they miss the joy of being led by the Spirit.

We must take Galatians 5:4 seriously. *"If you are trying to make yourself right with God by keeping the law, you have been cut off from Christ! You have fallen away from God's grace"*. (NLT). Only one tiny effort to validate ourselves in terms of the law is enough to invalidate grace in our lives and to cut us off from Christ! If young Christians are made to submit to the law until such time as they are mature enough, they will never mature. Law keeping does not bring about maturity; maturity is measured by faith, and our faith grows stronger in tandem with our understanding of grace.

In the same passage, Paul clarifies who guardianship is intended for: *"Until faith in Christ was shown to us as the way of becoming right with God, we were guarded by the law. We were kept in protective custody, so to speak, until we could put our faith in the coming Savior"* (Galatians 3:23 NLT). From these words, it is clear that the guardianship of the law ended when faith was revealed through the coming of Jesus.

So many believers have gotten so accustomed to living underprivileged, that they're not even aware that they're missing out on anything. With misinformation, they have learnt to accept things as they are, thus foregoing their rightful grace privileges. Often well-meant sermons proclaim a grace that is conditional, and tragically, that's all it takes to disinherit innocent believers.

It is vitally important that, a Covenant validated with blood, is not compromised with a second attempt at validating it with feeble strivings at law keeping. By adding conditions, rightful inheritances are simply forfeited. Bequests can only be apportioned by faith!

Seeing that the New Covenant replaced the Old Covenant, in so far as born again believers are concerned, should we be bothering with any Old Testament writings in our daily walk? We most certainly should! If we liken the cross to a tea strainer, and the Old Testament to a pot of tea, then the liquid that gets through the strainer is the part of the Old Testament that we continue to use. The tealeaves left in the strainer are the Old Testament requirements that were fulfilled on our behalf on the cross. Once fulfilled by Jesus, they need never be fulfilled again. The mere effort of trying to re-fulfil them is insulting to the One who went to so much trouble and pain to fulfil them for us—He paid very dearly for our liberation.

The Lie

For the enemy to cancel our inheritances, he doesn't have to get us to do some heinous sin. All he has to do is get us to work for God's favour. He knows that our failed efforts will induce a sense of shame that will make us vulnerable to his accusations. He takes every opportunity to attack our sense of worthiness, using shame to bring our prayers into question. With the law, we can never be quite sure that we have done enough, and Satan uses such uncertainty to sow doubt into our prayers—it's how he disinherits us.

All the many wonderful truths that we receive Sunday after Sunday are wasted on us, if we are basing our entitlement to them upon the shaky foundation of our worthiness—on this basis, we are dead in the water, without the slightest hope of inheriting anything at all!

"Get real Deon", you might be protesting. Believe me, I have lived close enough to the purveyors of the "holiness" message. I have yet to meet one who is capable of keeping the laws they so passionately proclaim. These people are easily offended, but, as they say in the classics, "people in glass houses should not throw stones".

Guilt, the Reward for Keeping the Law

For merely trying to make ourselves right by keeping one law, we make ourselves guilty of all the law (James 2:10). For example, if we try and keep the ninth commandment not to lie, one slip of the tongue will make us guilty of all ten commandments.

The moral of the story is: Do not keep any Old Covenant law whatsoever—it's "the law of sin and death" (Rom 8:2 KJV). The law of life in Christ Jesus is the only law worth keeping. It is accessed by faith in response to His love.

Though Jesus rescued us from the curse of the law of sin and death, so many attempt to get into God's good books through law keeping. Sadly, this practice can only return them to the very same curses from which they have been rescued. Either they throw their hands up in exasperation and give up, or they try all the harder—attempting to keep even more laws to make up for the ones they failed to keep— anything to escape the curses. Unfortunately, this is how curses are perpetuated—a vicious cycle of desperation, leading nowhere except to disinheritance. To compromise grace with the tiniest degree of law, is to bring a curse upon oneself.

The Law is Sin's Best Friend

Paul said, *"The law gives sin its power"* (1 Cor 15:56 NLT). Sounds wrong, doesn't it? If sin is our enemy then it follows that the law is also our enemy—according to this scripture, the law empowers sin. The slightest vestige of law keeping is diabolical, harmful, destructive, detrimental and disinheriting! We simply cannot afford the negative consequences of turning to the law for our righteousness.

Embedded in every person is his or her personal nature. We may teach a pig to behave like a sheep, but the moment it sees mud, its old embedded nature forces it to roll in the sloppy muck. It cannot help itself.

We can domesticate a bull, and it will act like a poodle until someone waves a red flag; suddenly its old embedded nature takes over, and the best we can do is to run for cover.

If we think that we have successfully modified our behaviour, beware; our embedded nature is apt to rise to the surface when least expected. Whenever we are told not to do something, the urge to do it intensifies. It's in our nature—it's what the red flag is to the bull. *"Sin took advantage of the law and aroused all kinds of forbidden desires within me! If there were no law sin would not have that power"* (Rom 7:8 NLT).

I saw this in my small children. They had no interest in a pair of scissors lying idly on the coffee table. But, as any good parent would, we told them not to touch them. That's all it took to arouse a desire to touch them. Once aroused, it became difficult to prize the pair of scissors out of their tiny fingers. For some crazy reason the words "Thou shalt not" arouses all kinds of opposite desires within us.

When I was young, picking fruit from the trees in our neighbour's garden, under the cover of darkness, was a lot more fun than picking fruit from our own trees. Why? Because it was forbidden!

The very sin that is preached against, is the sin that will manifest in our behaviour—it intensifies the temptation. Fighting the urge to sin does not reduce sin; it empowers sin!

Without realising it, some preachers have been known to lay their personal hang-ups on congregants—soon their hang-ups become everybody's hang-ups. In the process, everybody becomes preoccupied with the very things that are forbidden.

"The letter killeth, but the spirit giveth life" (2Co 3:6). People wither and wilt when fed on the bad news of the law of sin and death, but thrive and blossom on the good news of God's grace! What a glorious gospel we have—so much to celebrate! And it is infinitely more edifying than moping over our shortcomings.

Jesus did not just come to give us a good example to emulate; He is the very image and prototype of what a believer is. We are the spitting image of Him. He deposited Himself within us. In our discovery of His beauty, we discover our beauty!

We are often encouraged to strive to be more like Jesus. In light of the fact that no-one ever gets it right, it would seem that we may have missed the point.

If I were to tell a person that there is no need to strive to be like Jesus, because they are already as glorious as Him, I would in all likelihood, be accused of blasphemy! Of course, my words carry little weight, but they are not my words; they are Jesus', and that puts an entirely different spin to them. In John 17:22 Jesus said that He has given us the glory His Father gave Him. That being the case, we cannot know our glory until we have gotten to know His glory—it resides within us!

This crucial discovery puts an end to the futility of striving to be like Him. Although we can't do it; Christ within us can! But for as long as we allow prejudice and offense taking to dominate our thoughts and actions, we deny Him the privilege of living His values through our actions.

Nothing could be more beautiful than a person beaming from within with the glory of Jesus! Let's face it, nobody can do a better job of being like Jesus than Jesus Himself. His living is always right living—the fruit of the Spirit in action!

We ought to leave judgemental preaching to the "accuser of the brethren"—he is a past master at discrediting believers. Let us not make his job any easier.

As has already been mentioned; in order to define a believer, one needs to define Jesus. Why does religion keep this vital information from us? Often religion sends us on a wild goose chase to become something that we already are. When it becomes obvious that we can't achieve it, we settle for pretence—it's okay when everybody else is also pretending. Really?

If each denomination has a different behavioural code, then it is obvious that all such codes are flawed. Religion often attaches enormous value to religious achievements, positions and titles. If we have allowed religion to define us by our actions, then we have been deceived. We are defined in heavenly terms—we are what Jesus is!

Self-glorifying titles do not impress God. We are His sons and daughters, and that outranks every religious title ever dreamed up. And that includes the most glorified title known to mankind—the exalted title of "Pope". At the precise moment of rebirth, every new born believer outranks any such contrived religious status.

Don't get me wrong, achievements are great—they just don't define who we are. Law keeping achievements matter even less! Fortunately, we are defined in terms of "who we belong to". God reveals our value in Jesus' value; nothing that we dare to add to the value we already have in Him can make us one iota more glorious or more righteous. And by the same token, nothing that we do or don't do can subtract from our glory and righteousness. Our glory and righteousness were established and defined in Christ's glory and righteousness—it has nothing to do with our achievements and everything to do with His achievements!

One of my previous pastors took a particularly hard line on an ex-worship leader who had chosen an alternative lifestyle. Although he had left the church, the pastor still took measures to publicly ostracise him. He asked the congregation to stand up and make a public declaration, putting him out of fellowship, handing his body over to Satan so that his soul could be saved.

Although he could find scripture for this, it seems that he did not take Matthew 18:17 into account. It states that we are to treat such a brother as a heathen. The question is—how should the church be treating heathen? Surely not by ostracizing them! Afterall, is the church's mission really about me, we and us? Isn't it supposed to be about laying our lives down for heathen? What was the example that Jesus set for us to emulate? Was it to be "me" focused, or "others" focused? Afterall, isn't it true to say that the church is the only institution that exists for the benefit of non-members? Shouldn't we be welcoming them with open arms?

The worse the sin, the more the church is needed to show grace. This is the only way that the church can continue to have a positive influence on our fallen brethren. Sure, the brother needs to know what God has to say about his choices, but outside of grace, there is simply no other way to restore him.

We simply don't have what it takes to bring about personal change. Fortunately, grace, the most powerful force in the universe, initiates change at heart level. Excommunication in and of itself does not possess any power, except the power to alienate people from the very help they so desperately need. Unfortunately, excommunication does possess the power to injure others, and in turn, back-fire on those involved in making such harsh judgements. This man died in a motor accident shortly after this incident.

Instead of cleansing the worship team, this Pharisaic attitude aroused sin within the team in the years that followed. The next worship team leader walked out of her marriage to run away with the team's guitarist. She was married to one of our pastors. He was immediately forced to step down from office—another ungracious church government blunder. She married the guitarist, then divorced him to have an affair with her sister's husband. They married and subsequently divorced. Sadly, she died of cancer a short while later.

Two worship team members and a youth pastor chose alternative lifestyles. An associate pastor left, then divorced and later died. One of the musicians was rumoured to have been involved in serious fraud. Another associate pastor had an affair. Our subsequent senior pastor had an adulterous affair with one of our lady pastors, destroying both of their careers. He subsequently committed suicide.

This church did not get this way because it was lax on moral teaching and control. To the contrary, it was extremely strong on chastity, virtue, moral standards, repentance, and godliness. Where did they go wrong then? Control is where they went wrong—unfortunately, pure grace loses its power to influence lives for the better when diluted with conditions, regardless of how morally sound they may seem.

By excluding grace, they had excluded God from the process. Sin took advantage of the strong demand for virtue and morality. The higher the demand to stop sinning, the higher the temptation to sin. *"But sin took advantage of this law and aroused all kinds of forbidden desires within me! If there were no law, sin would not have that power."* The more we're controlled by commandments, the more we're enticed into sin. Law is harmful to our spiritual wellbeing. In this church, control and the over emphasis of moral codes, led to the moral collapse of its leadership.

What shall we say about the law then? Is it bad? Did God do something bad when He gave it to Moses? Of course not; the law is holy and good (Gal 7:12). The law is the schoolmaster that revealed my inability to make myself right before God. It revealed my desperate need to find another solution. Jesus offers that solution—a state of permanent righteousness, gloriously unaffected by our penchant for sinning. Something that is only obtainable through faith.

When we strive to keep the law, we are apt to compare ourselves with others who may not be quite as law abiding as ourselves. Judging them is every bit as sinful as the sin we judge. Unfortunately, the law has this "haughtifying" effect on people.

Who would want to be able to boast that he or she is the least sinful of all sinners in Hell? Nobody, I am sure. In that case, don't strive for righteousness through law keeping. You will end up proud, judgemental and disinherited!

Sin Conscious or God Conscious?

The devil wants us to be sin conscious rather than God conscious. How does he achieve this? He keeps us trying to fulfil at least part of the law, knowing full well that we will fail in our quest, and that our failure will produce a sense of shame. God has a better plan for us. He fulfilled all the law for us, and allowed us to go straight through the Temple veil into His presence. From God's side, there is no condemnation upon believers.

So many Christians live in self-condemnation. Imagine the victory they would experience if they got to know that the Father loves them in their sin as much as He loves Jesus in His perfection! He will not love them any more deeply if they stop sinning, nor love them any less if they don't. God does not just give love—He is love!

It's a human tendency: We tend to expect more of ourselves than God expects of us. But He is not looking for perfection—He is more realistic than that—more aware of our propensity to sin than we are. He is profoundly aware that sanctification is a lifelong process—a task that can only be carried out by the Sanctifier Himself. Try as we may, we all leave this planet in an imperfect state. In that case, what does God expect from us? He expects fruitfulness. Can we be fruitful without being perfect? Most certainly. Jacob and David were fruitful yet far from perfect. Fruitfulness is not what we do; it's what the Holy Spirit does—He bears luscious fruit through us; despite our many imperfections—imperfections are common to all.

The Impossibility of fulfilling the Law

Other than Jesus, there has never been one single person who has ever managed to keep the whole law. If it is that far out of reach—what makes us think that we will be the first to achieve it? If keeping the law is impossible to mankind, God may as well have commanded us to jump over the moon to qualify. No matter how hard we may try, we are never going to be able to do it. The moon is hundreds of thousands of kilometres away.

I might be able to jump one metre, and you might be able to jump one and a half metres, but both of us are still thousands of kilometres short of the moon. My aging mother could manage a quarter metre and an Olympic high jumper, two metres, but where does that leave them? If we choose to try to keep the law to stay saved, or to gain God's approval, no matter how close we get to perfection, none of us are making it.

Now Jesus has gone to the moon and back for us (metaphorically speaking), so that we don't have to do it ourselves. Although we cannot make it over the moon, you can be sure that the one who can jump one and a half metres, will look down his nose upon the one who can only manage one metre. Unfortunately, human nature, being what it is, is prone to measure itself against others, and end up with smugness and condescension. The moral of the story is not to keep any "law of sin and death" (Romans 8:2). There is a new law that is written on the tables of our hearts—it is the still small voice of the Holy Spirit, who has promised to lead and to guides us.

HOW CAN WE EXPERIENCE GOD'S GRACE?

His grace is so markedly different to human thinking that it takes a special grant of spiritual enlightenment to understand the enormity of it. *"I pray also that the eyes of your heart may be enlightened in order that you may know the hope to which he has called you, the riches of his glorious inheritance in the saints"* (Eph 1:18 NIV).

There will always be more to God's love than we have experienced. It's so big that it is always over and beyond anything we could ever imagine. Participation in His grace will always be limited to the grace concepts we have inherited. That being the case, what can we do to improve our participation? Fortunately, it has nothing to do with our performance, and everything to do with what we understand of His goodness towards us.

It is only natural for flawed humanity to feel unworthy in the presence of a holy God. But once His unconditional love has instilled value within us, there is no further place for such feelings.

Feelings of unworthiness are profoundly limiting! Before we know it, we have scaled down in expectation, and settled for unremarkable living. So much of the church has settled for a wishy-washy gospel. We need divine help to understand how wide, how long, how high and how deep His love for us really is!

The concept of agape love is so exceedingly different to any of our earthly points of reference. Clearly, it is difficult to wrap our minds around a concept that exceeds our experiences. Also, it doesn't sit well with the society we live in—we live by an ethic of reward. It is only natural to grant honour and respect to those who are worthy of it. But that's certainly not what grace is!

Our particular concepts of love have been shaped by life's experiences. And everybody's experiences are unique and different. Relationships with friends, mentors, family, and more especially, with our earthly fathers have shaped our concepts of God's fatherly love towards us. It's not easy to come to grips with concepts that exceed our experiences. Paradigms are not easily shifted.

Clearly, trust is gained by promises fulfilled. If, in our individual experiences, promises are seldom kept, we will in all likelihood apply that limitation to our prayers, thus bringing an element of certainty to them. We won't have the gumption to be emphatic in faith!

According to James, if our faith waivers, our prayers are rendered powerless. Clearly, our degree of trust is closely aligned to our understanding of God's love for us. In getting to know Him better, we get to trust Him more—faith thrives on trust!

To the degree of our understanding of God's love for us, we experience divine power and fullness of life (Eph. 3:19). Without doubt, everybody desires fullness of life—the grandest prize of all! Sadly, most Christians never get to experience it. Depression, boredom, worry, lack and sickness are certainly not fullness of life. There is so much more to life. But sadly, no-one experiences God's grace privileges beyond the limits they have set for His grace!

However good we have come to believe God to be; there is always more of His goodness yet to be discovered—eternity is not long enough to discover all. His good intentions towards us are beyond imagination. But with the help of the Holy Spirit, we can progressively get to know more and more of it—a never-ending journey. Clearly, it is not humanly possible to know all of something that is infinite. Imagine: Eternity will be spent in awe of an endless unfolding of His goodness (Eph 1:18).

So, if we were to assume that God loves us for what we have done, how could we ever be sure that we have not done something else to cause Him to stop loving us?

Seeing that we did nothing to cause Him to love us in the first place, nothing else that we may do or not do could cause Him to stop loving us. He started this love affair without our permission. *"And I am convinced that nothing can ever separate us from his love. Death can't, and life can't. The angels can't, and the demons can't. Our fears for today, our worries about tomorrow, and even the powers of hell can't keep God's love away"* (Rom 8:38, 39 NLT).

In the same way that He did not expect us to clean up our acts before saving us, He does not expect us to clean up our acts before healing us, providing for us or favouring us. We don't get blessed for what we have done; we get blessed for what He has done! It takes nothing more than faith to invoke His favour.

He loves us just as we are with all of our nasty quirks, shortcomings and sins, and wants us to feel the same about ourselves. But how can we love ourselves while sinful? A good question! Well here's the deal—God loves us! He has a blind spot—He cannot see our sins (metaphorically speaking). That doesn't mean that He won't help us overcome our penchant for sinning, it's just that He doesn't count our sins against us—He has already counted them against Jesus, and Jesus has dispensed with them on the cross! If we can love ourselves exactly as we are right now, in the way that God does, change will follow, not because of our ardent strivings, but because we begin to see ourselves the way He sees us—pure, righteous, undefiled and infinitely lovable! Humanity has a way of living up to the image it has formed of itself.

The thought that God loves us regardless is immensely liberating. When the dark cloud of condemnation lifts, the pathway leading to practical righteousness comes into focus. In getting to understand the extent of His love for us, we get to understand our personal significance and value. Knowing that He loves us, warts and all, opens the way for us to feel the same about ourselves and others.

What is so important about loving ourselves you may ask? The answer is that we can only love God and others to the degree that we love ourselves. Jesus said it in so many words when He said that we are to love others as much as we love ourselves. The reason that He didn't tell us to love them more than ourselves is because it is simply not possible to give more love than we have found for ourselves.

Think of ourselves as jugs. We always make place in our hearts for those who love us. The thought that God could find us lovable gives us sufficient reason to make more room for Him. Thereafter, character shaping follows without effort. Once filled with His love, we contain something of value to pour out to others.

When we come to accept that we are loved despite our less than perfect behaviour, it becomes possible to love others despite their less than perfect behaviour. The wonderful thing about finding value for ourselves, is that we overflow, gushing value and worth onto others. It is not that we try to make it happen; it's that God's grace towards us makes it happen. To encounter such individuals, is to encounter Him—their presence exudes His presence!

True grace is not charm; true love simply cannot be contrived. Real love edifies, uplifts and encourages without trying. It is so natural that we are often not even aware that we are making a positive difference to those around us. Ultimately, we are only capable of giving value to others to the extent that we have found value for ourselves. Without it, we have nothing to offer.

Whenever we are tempted to belittle ourselves for our stupidity, we should bear in mind that Jesus never does. Even if we have done something dreadful, we remain righteous in His sight. We are exactly who He says we are—the righteousness of God in Christ.

How does God's Love differ from Ours?

Compare these two different kinds of love:

Our kind of love	God's kind of love
• Conditional love.	• Unconditional love.
• Responds with love when loved.	• Initiates love.
• Loves less when hated.	• Loves despite being hated.
• Reacts with unkindness when confronted with unkindness.	• Unfazed by unkindness.

• Needs a reason to love.	• Loves without reason.
• Loves those who deserve it.	• Loves whether deserving or not.
• Is easily offended when wronged.	• Takes no offence when wronged.

As believers, our form of love is often tinged with hidden agendas and self-interest. Whenever these two types of "love" are mixed, we end up with a bad blend. Agape is not agape when it is not purely agape. Believers give love mixed in various proportions—seldom able to keep agape purely agape. But with God there is never a mixture. Of this we can be certain; His love for us is always the same—unaffected by our performance, whether good or bad.

He fore-knew that, no matter how good He was to His children, they would forever be disappointing Him. But not even that was reason enough to prevent Him from laying His life down for them. His love does not increase or decrease in accordance with their conduct. It's always the same. We always know exactly where we stand with Him.

Sin does not reduce grace; sin is the very reason for extending grace. If it were not for our sin, mercy and grace would serve no purpose. His love is the central theme of His grace. He has made up His mind to love us regardless, and nothing, not even our sinning can cause to Him change His mind about loving us!

Why is God pursuing us with His goodness? It is because we are His dearly loved children, and spoiling their children is a fatherly delight. As much as earthly dads love their children, our heavenly Dad loves His children, only infinitely more!

Let's settle this once and for all: God's goodness and grace can never be deserved. Even if it were vaguely possible to deserve grace, grace would no longer be grace; it would be reward—a payment for work done.

"*For if you are trying to make yourself right with God by trying to keep the law, you have been cut off from Christ! You have fallen away from God's grace*". (Gal 5:4 NLT). Cut off from Christ? Is this really possible? Will we really be cut off from Him for innocently trying to deserve His love? Believe me, if that's what His word says, then it is so!

"*So if you claim that God's promise is for those who obey God's law and think they are good enough in God's sight, then you are saying that faith is useless. And in that case the promise is also meaningless*" (Rom 4:14 NLT). Can this be right? Can I really render my faith useless by merely obeying the law? That's a bit harsh isn't it? What does the next verse say? "*But the law brings punishment on those who try to obey it. The only way to avoid breaking the law is to have no law to break*" (Rom 4:15 NLT). Will I really be punished for innocently "trying" to obey the law? Won't He see my good intentions? Afterall, I am doing it in an effort to please Him. Sorry—His word is the final authority! The law will definitely bring punishment on me. One law added to grace, disqualifies grace altogether—it's that simple!

What part does Faith Play?

Seeing that we cannot receive anything from God through our own merits, how should we go about receiving from Him? It is by faith and faith alone! We can pray and fast until we are blue in the face. We can attend all the church meetings in town. We can feed the poor and homeless, and care for widows and orphans. We can be deacons or elders, worship team leaders or youth leaders. We can speak in tongues, prophecy and witness to the lost. As good as all these are, they don't give us leverage with God—His favour is not for sale—it can only be received by faith.

We see it again and again in Jesus' ministry—it was people's faith that got His attention—nothing else triggered the miraculous. It was not their sin or their lack of law keeping that prevented Jesus from doing any great miracles in Nazareth; it was purely their unbelief.

He chided some for their little faith, and commended others for their great faith. Would you agree with me that it takes great faith to walk on water? Surprisingly, after Peter had walked on water, Jesus chided him for his *"little faith"*. On another occasion, after calming the sea He said, *"O ye of little faith"* to his beloved disciples, but when a pagan Roman Centurion asked Him to just speak the word and his servant would be healed, Jesus said, *"He had never seen such great faith"*.

The centurion, being a non-Jew, did not keep the law, yet Jesus granted him his request on the basis of his faith alone. In fact, Jesus was so moved by his faith that He said that it was greater than any faith He had encountered in Israel. Israelites were law keepers, but none of them were healed on the basis of their law keeping. As surprising as it may seem, not even a state of sinlessness, if that were remotely possible, would lend any weight to our prayers.

For faith to be effective, it must meet with grace; not with law. Faith in maybe's, if's and but's is powerless faith. Faith works with certainties, and nothing is more certain than the grace of God. Once we have applied our faith to God's graciousness, there is nothing more to be done—that's because the rest is for God's account.

Prayers don't get answered by reason of our worthiness; prayers get answered by reason of unshakable confidence. Confidence has the audacity to declare that a prayer has been answered before there is even the slightest evidence of an answer! Once faith has been applied, nothing more is required of us, except to patiently wait for materialisation!

If God were to answer our prayers based on our ability to comply with the law, or any other churchified rules, nobody's prayers would ever get answered— *"there is none righteous, no not one"*—not one in the entire history of mankind! (Rom 3:10).

When we are expecting to be favoured in response to something good we have done, we are obviously not expecting to be favoured for something good God has done. Unless our faith is founded upon His goodness, our faith is misplaced, and without faith it is impossible to please God!

Our boast of law keeping does not go down well with God. It must be awfully disappointing for Him to see His generosity being spurned by the very ones He went out of His way to win over with love. Our very best attempt to repay Him for His priceless kindness, would be an insult. Even a lifetime's accumulation of wealth, would be a payment far short of the price He paid for us. Any such thinking would trivialize the cross. Never forget the cost Jesus paid for our welfare. To turn to law keeping, would be to slam the door in His face. He wants to do so much more for us, but our feeble strivings to repay Him with works, reduces His gift into a purchase. And His love is not for sale!

He has done so much to convince us, yet we don't seem to get it— our accomplishments are a work of the flesh and count for naught. It takes faith alone to unlock grace. We dare not take any credit for any contribution we have made—all the credit belongs to Him and Him alone—they are His accomplishments; not ours! Trying to make ourselves worthy of His favour may seem harmless enough, but why would anyone strive for something that cancels grace?

We have been invited to enter the throne room of grace to ask for help in time of need. But for those who would dare to enter on the basis of their law keeping achievements, they must contend with a sense of unworthiness—a faith disabling roadblock. The kingdom requires nothing short of unflinching confidence—it takes boldfaced assuredness to unlock our inheritances.

When we know that we are in right standing with God, an inexplicable confidence follows. If Jesus was clear on anything, it was that it takes this kind of confidence to unlock the promises. Any right making attempts on our part, serve only to introduce a sense of uncertainty to our prayers. There is always an unanswered question in the minds of those who strive for His favour. It is a question for which nobody seems to have an answer, "Have I done enough?" This kind of indecisiveness immobilises faith. If we are wondering whether or not our prayers will be answered, they will not be answered! It's that simple!

It is different for those who know their identity in Christ. Their right-standing with God reinforces their confidence. The good news is that none of our failings and shortcomings affect our identity. Our identity is in Christ's significance; not ours! We did not achieve a sinless identity for not sinning. No, a spotless identity was handed to us on a silver platter. It is based on Christ's lack of sin; not ours!

So, God's word settles the question of our right-standing once and for all. We are already the righteousness of God in Christ. We are already seated together with Christ Jesus in heavenly places. We are already brand-new creatures that did not exist before rebirth—creatures born of incorruptible seed—incapable of being contaminated by sin for the rest of our lives.

But in reality, as much as we would prefer not to, we cannot deny that we continue to sin. Here's the secret: We ought not to confuse our practical righteousness with our positional righteousness. Positional righteousness is not something that can be achieved, and that's why God does not require us to produce a résumé of good works to commend ourselves. His grace is enough!

To understand our relationship, is to understand our identity. We do not relate to Him in terms of our performance; we relate to him in terms of a covenant signed in blood. Our praiseworthy performances do not even enter the equation.

How is Obedience Connected to Grace?

Often Christians equate grace with disobedience. For this reason, they remain sceptical of it. This leaves them to strive in their own strength to be holy, consigning themselves to religious servitude, thus foregoing their blood bought state of rest!

So where does obedience fit in? Although every person since Adam has had the right to choose between obedience and disobedience, disobedience comes with a high price tag. Unless we are obedient to the promptings of the Holy Spirit, how will we be guided into the privilege and favour He has prepared for us? If anyone knows what is good for us, it is God, and He has a plan to guide us into more and more of His favour. Seeing that the Holy Spirit is leading us into favour, we need to be ready and eager to follow His instructions without hesitation. Our inheritances are at stake!

The question is: what should we be obedient to? The laws that were cast in stone, or the laws of God written on hearts of flesh? The answer is, those written on our hearts alone. (Jer 31:33,34 & Heb 8:8-12).

The Holy Spirit speaks to us from within with a still small voice. The problem is that we cannot hear His still small voice while it is being drowned out by well-meant, yet condemnatory preaching. Wherever there is law, there is judgement, and wherever there is judgement, there is condemnation and shame. Of course, this is a generalisation—it does not apply to churches that impart God's love as unconditionally as He does.

For as long as morality is controlled by pharisees, the moral guidance of the Holy Spirit will remain side-lined. By and large the church is reluctant to relinquish its role as moral policemen—reluctant to entrust congregants to the impeccable guidance of the Holy Spirit. Sadly, moral policing doesn't change hearts. With unchanged hearts, congregants have no option but to do their best to appear to be holy! When curses are borrowed from the Old Covenant to frighten them out of their sin, a spirit of subservience soon sets in. Although done with the best of intentions, it is nevertheless error. Can you imagine how God must feel when His shepherds terrorise His sheep? Sadly, His beloved children are often disinherited by the very messengers commissioned to lead them into their inheritances.

When the law is misused to keep members in line, what good does it actually achieve? Zero! When it promotes striving, people miss grace, thereby missing God's favour. Striving leads to a sense of self-sufficiency, if successful and defeat, if not. Neither outcome leads to inheritance. Self-sufficiency succeeds only in blocking God's all-sufficiency—a serious error! Quite obviously, no church would purposely set out to disinherit its members—yet legalistic demands upon congregants cannot achieve anything better.

The archangel told Mary that she would bear a son who would be the Saviour of the world. Humanly speaking, this was not possible. She had not had sexual relations with a man. Nevertheless, she responded, *"Be it unto me according to thy word"*. Her obedience resulted in a supernatural manifestation. As with her, our obedient responses cause grace to manifest in miracles. We do not get access to grace by virtue of our performances; we get access by virtue of our faith. Faith responds in obedience, saying, *"Be it unto me according to thy word"*.

When the wine ran out at a wedding reception, Mary said to the organisers *"Do whatever He tells you to do"*. Herein lies the key to moving from self-effort into grace. Grace achieves what would normally be impossible. The secret is to immediately respond with complete obedience, without the slightest hesitation!

Yogi, our spaniel, loved to go "walkies". The moment I put my walking shoes on, she would start yapping excitedly. She would even pick up on the word, "walk" when casually mentioned in conversation. She would fetch her leash, shaking it enthusiastically.

On the walk, she would run here, there and everywhere, but be restrained by me on the other end of her leash. In the process, she would choke as her collar constricted her breathing to the point of sounding asthmatic. As small as she was, I was forced to lean against her pull; doing my best to restrain her. If I had let her go, she would most likely have run into the traffic and gotten run over.

A trained dog doesn't need a leash. He acts on every word that his master speaks. When his master says "stay", he stays, and "walk", he walks—ever at his master's side, sensitive to his slightest gestures—

taking pleasure in obeying his master. He does not use his freedom from the leash to run into the traffic.

The Old Covenant had mankind on a short leash; jerking them back into line, keeping them from harming themselves. There were rewards for obedience, and curses for disobedience—the blessings motivating, and the curses restraining. Conversely the New Covenant of grace has no leash to keep us in check. We have the freedom to run into the traffic and get hurt, but the love of God constrains us, wooing us to voluntarily submit in obedience to His voice.

When we truly understand grace, our eyes and ears are ever alert and watchful, waiting and eager to attend to our Master's every desire. We are free to be disobedient, but we know that obedience comes with a handsome payoff—keeping us out of danger and leading us into greater blessings.

Love given with eagerness conveys so much more sincerity than love simply given because it is expected of believers. Legalism expects so much from us. But when love is not something we must do, but rather something we want to do, there is joy, both for the giver and for the receiver.

Divine lovers really want to be in each other's company. This kind of relationship was not possible under the Old Covenant's obligations and restraints. But under the New Covenant it is decidedly different—we are ever mindful of our Father, and He of us—each taking great delight in pleasing the other.

Our Lack is God's Opportunity

When our prayers go unanswered, we may feel the need to do a little more religion—anything to get God's attention. Big mistake! It's not by works lest any man should boast. Grace is not just one of the ways of solving the sin problem, it is God's one and only way!

If we don't have natural gifts, get supernatural gifts without charge.

If we can't be like Christ, let Christ within us be like Christ.

If we can't do what Christ would do, let Christ who is within us do what He would do.

If we lack abilities, get Christ's abilities.

If we lack health, get Christ's health.

If we lack provisions, get Christ's provisions.

If we lack joy, get the joy of the Lord.

If we lack peace, get the peace of God that passes all understanding.

If we have no plan for our lives, get God's plan for our lives.

If we feel that we lack personal holiness, rest in Christ's holiness.

Want any of God's stuff? Receive it free of charge—it simply cannot be earned—in fact, striving for it will keep you from it! Divine inheritances are available and awaiting collection. Sometimes, we want something so badly that we make all kinds of promises to God, hoping to impress Him with pious deal making. Ever wondered why He is not impressed? It is simple! Grace is not for sale! It can only be received without payment. Sadly, our best efforts serve only to disqualify us!

Not all church leaders have a clear understanding of the concept and scope of grace. As ropey as their ideas may be, it does not reflect poorly on them—we are all growing in our understanding of grace.

Pastors desire what's best for their flocks—they want them to turn their backs on sin—a commendable ideal! Their sincerity is not in question; it is the "how to" that is in question. Sadly, in urging congregants to produce fruit of the Spirit, they end up counterfeiting

His fruit. Only the Spirit can produce His fruit, anything less is plain and simply a forgery—a work of the flesh. It is not up to us to produce it; it is up to us to allow Him to produce it through us.

It is all about perspectives. From the perspective of grace, we regard our strengths as weaknesses and our virtues as shortcomings. Because we cannot manufacture His fruit, we must rely entirely on the Holy Spirit—His brand of fruit can only be produced by Him. All He requires of us is to surrender to His guidance. What about good works then? Good works will follow, almost as if by accident.

When supermarket shopping, we trust certain brands because they deliver consistent quality. Our very best efforts to produce fruit of the Spirit can only produce works of the flesh—its quality cannot be trusted. However, the brand of fruit produced by the Holy Spirit can always be relied upon for quality. Sadly, in our efforts to produce fruit of the Spirit, we end up counterfeiting it—it's the best we can do.

James, in his letter, talks about showing our faith by our works, but Paul in his letter to the Romans tells us that we cannot achieve anything through works. Does this sound like a contradiction? Not at all. We cannot get saved or favoured by working for it. But once we have it, we can use our new found faith to produce good works. We are not saved by good works; we are saved "unto good works"!

If you received a computer as a birthday gift, you cannot claim to have paid for it, but the fact that you are sending emails is undeniable proof that you have a computer. In the same way that emails are evidence of a computer, good works are evidence of salvation.

If we set out to do good works simply to prove that we are people of faith, we will prove absolutely nothing. Even unbelievers can do good works—many of them live exemplary lives. Some do as many good works as believers. In the same way that good works done by unsaved people cannot save them; good works done by saved people cannot keep them saved.

If we are doing good works to prove our faith, rather than as a consequence of our faith, then our hearts might need further divine adjustment. How do we get our hearts adjusted? All it takes is a better understanding of how unconditionally we are loved.

Some have said that James' reference to show our works by our faith proves that sinful works can stand in the way of our prayers being answered. But James clarified this misunderstanding by giving us two examples: Both Abraham and Rahab were credited with righteousness, not for repenting from sin, but for deeds that demonstrated their faith.

Abraham's good work was his obedience to sacrifice his son, and Rahab's good work was to hide the spies and help them escape. Neither of these deeds involved dealing with their sin. Rahab was a prostitute. Clearly, James was not making a point for sin being able to prevent our prayers from being answered.

Interestingly, Abraham was not granted righteousness when he obeyed God's instruction to sacrifice Isaac. He was granted righteousness much earlier—it happened when he believed that he would be the father of many nations. The good deeds that James referred to were not acts of holiness; they were acts of faith.

If we misunderstand this point and think that our prayers will go unanswered because there is sin in our lives, our prayers will definitely not be answered. We might as well play a game of tennis—it would benefit us a whole lot more than trying to get our prayers answered by virtue of our piety.

If, when praying for a person, we were to tell that person that they cannot expect answers to prayer while there is sin in their lives, we are aiding and abetting Satan, disinheriting sincere followers of Jesus. In

Jesus' healing ministry, He never once made any such suggestion. Our misunderstanding on this point becomes a prayer blocking tool in Satan's hands.

You may think that there is sin and there is SIN! One more prayer blocking than another. Then I must ask you to define the difference. At what point does ordinary sin become prayer blocking SIN? One lie, two lies, three lies? You might say that one lie now and again is different to being a habitual liar. Really? The word of God makes no such distinction. On this point it is clear; one tiny lie would make us guilty of the whole law. And nobody could be guiltier than that!

If habitual sin could withhold God's blessings, then Jesus was out of line when He healed all who asked for healing. Never once did He even broach the subject of repentance before healing them. We are expected to emulate Jesus, and as such, would do well not to imply that healing is conditional. To do so, would make us complicit—aiding and abetting Satan in his quest to block believers' inheritances.

This being the case, why did Peter state, *"For the eyes of the Lord are over the righteous, and his ears are open unto their prayers: but the face of the Lord is against them that do evil"*? (1Pe 3:12 KJV). We must ask ourselves, "At what point do we cross the line into evil?" This is a hard question for law keepers to answer—the holiness they seek is unattainable. Seeing that all believers fall short of the glory of God, it should be obvious that believers are not the evil ones referred to in this scripture.

For people of grace it is different—they are led by the Spirit. *"This I say then, Walk in the Spirit, and ye shall not fulfil the lust of the flesh"* (Gal 5:16 KJV).

BODY, SOUL AND SPIRIT

If God is holy and I am not, then what do I have to do to measure up? A predicament that has bewildered mankind throughout the ages.

Fortunately, God does not deal with us on the basis of our personal conduct. He deals with us on the basis of who we are in Christ.

Most Christians have an identity crisis. Often people confuse what they do for a living with who they are. If you ask a man what he is, you are likely to get an answer like doctor, plumber or accountant. But what we do is not who we are. The same applies to Christians. Many evaluate themselves in terms of their Christian position or performance and not by who they are in Christ.

But God does not deal with us in accordance with our performance. From Adam, for two thousand five hundred years, He dealt with mankind according to mercy. From Moses, for one thousand five hundred years, He dealt with mankind according to the law. Then from the cross, for two thousand years, He once again deals with mankind according to mercy.

Why the law then? *"For as many as are of the works of the law are under the curse; for it is written, 'Cursed is everyone who does not continue in all things which are written in the book of the law, to do them'"* (Gal 3:10 KJV).

The law comes with many curses. If we have chosen to live under the law, we have chosen to be cursed—it's that simple! Even in the extreme unlikelihood of being able to keep 99% of the law, we would still be cursed. The slightest infringement invokes all the curses of Deuteronomy 28. Seeing that no-one in the history of mankind has ever managed to score 100%, the promised devastations would be inevitable.

If we approach God on the basis of our law keeping, we can never know whether or not we have done enough. Conversely, if we approach Him as sinful, yet justified by faith, we have met all the conditions.

"But that no one is justified by the law in the sight of God is evident, for 'the just shall live by faith'" (Gal 3:11 NKJV). From this, it is obvious that law cannot justify us—it wasn't given for that purpose. In fact, exactly the opposite applies. The law was given to make us guilty before God in the hope that we would turn to a Saviour.

Very often, law keepers find reason for smugness—a sense of being better than others—at times manifesting in religious haughtiness. Religion has a way of making decent people distasteful to others.

Much of the church has misused the law—urging people to keep it in order to gain God's approval, and to get their prayers answered. They say that God cannot use unholy vessels. Well here's the bottom line: God has no choice in the matter—all vessels are tainted with unholiness in one way or another. By His standard, we all fall short of His glory. Seeing that He has never once found a holy vessel, but has always used what was available, we can rest assured that soiled vessels are not disqualified.

Based on performance, there are no holy vessels, nor have there ever been, except for Jesus of course. Clearly, it is only by virtue of the mercies of God that we are able to approach Him, and never by virtue of our personal performance.

"Whatsoever is not of faith is sin" (Rom 14:23 KJV). *"The law is not of faith"* (Gal 3:12 KJV). It couldn't be clearer—law keeping for right standing with God is not of faith and therefore it is of sin. The very act of attempting to find justification through law keeping is sin in itself—it doesn't impute right-standing; it can only impute wrong-standing! If, however, we use the law for that for which it was intended, it is not sin.

In the recent past, the law has been stretched to include such things as, no movies, no smoking, no drinking, short hair for men, long hair for women, no makeup or slacks for women etc. The fact that the rules keep changing is proof enough of its folly. Keeping religiously invented legalistic rules is no different to attempting to make oneself right through Law keeping—the only difference is that legalisms requirements keep changing.

If we approach God based on any kind of rule keeping, it is plain and simply worthy of a curse. *"For as many as are of the works of the law are under the curse"* (Gal 3:10 KJV). It couldn't be plainer—there are no blessings for the part that we get right. With the Law we are either 100% perfect, or 100% cursed, and in desperate need of a Saviour. Fortunately, there is a Saviour who has suffered our curses for us and granted us His righteousness. There is no other way to escape the curses. *"Christ has redeemed us from the curse of the law, having become a curse for us"* (Gal 3:13 NKJV).

God did not introduce the law out of anger. Nor did He introduce it for us to attain holiness through keeping it; rather He gave it to show us what perfection is. If we are going to aim for salvation based on perfection, then we would have to be 100% perfect—a profoundly unachievable aspiration. Despair, the only reward awaiting anyone foolish enough to attempt it. Hopefully, despair will bring them to their senses and cause them to turn to God for His mercy and grace.

The law has another profitable purpose. The law shows us right from wrong. It is a benchmark against which I can measure my decisions. Although it doesn't possess the power to make me right; it does provide me with a yardstick. Obviously, God will never lead me contrary to the law.

In the mind of legalists, the nagging question is: "Does grace give us a licence to sin?" This question almost always crops up whenever the subject of grace is broached. If it does not crop up, then we should ask ourselves if we have really told it like it is—have we compromised it for fear of ruffling religious feathers? To legalistically indoctrinated minds, the unconditionality of grace is offensive. "How could blatant offenders be let off so easily? It has got to be heresy!" The concept of unconditional love is far too radical a concept—guaranteed to ruffle religious feathers. To them, it's far too soft on sin! Liberty seldom goes down well with legalists.

Paul's message of grace was so radical that he knew that he would have to contend with this question, so he pre-empted it with, *"What shall we say then? Shall we continue in sin, that grace may abound? God forbid. How shall we, that are dead to sin, live any longer therein?"* (Rom 6:1,2 KJV). Besides, why would believers wish to return to the very self-destructive muck from which they have been rescued? The thought of it just doesn't add up!

The law was not given for the purpose of earning favour; it was given to reveal that all people are condemned. In coming to grips with their sorry plight, they will hopefully seek a way out. Jesus has provided the one and only way out—He provided mercy and grace.

"For if the inheritance is of the law, it is no longer of promise; but God gave it to Abraham by promise". (Gal 3:18 NKJV). Abraham received his blessing by faith without any help from the law. And, thankfully, we receive Abraham's blessings in exactly the same way—by faith alone! Law keeping doesn't even enter the equation. We are included in Abraham's blessing by way of our relationship to Jesus. *"Now to Abraham and his Seed were the promises made. He does not say, 'And to seeds,' as of many, but as of one, 'And to your Seed,' who is Christ"* (Gal 3:16 NKJV).

As we saw earlier in Galatians 3:17, in Abraham's time there was no law to fulfil—the law only came about hundreds of years later, and when it arrived on the scene, it did not cancel the blessing of Abraham—his blessing sailed straight past the law's period of existence, and continues to apply, without requiring us to keep a single Old Covenant law.

At rebirth, a transformation of our spirit man took place. Our spirits are the core part of who we are—perfect in every sense, needing no further adjustment for all time and eternity. Unless we are thoroughly convinced that this is so, we will in all likelihood strive to change something that cannot be changed. Unless we grasp the implications of our royal identity as new creatures, we will not have the nerve to lay claim to our rightful royal inheritances. For the great majority of believers, their blood bought legacies simply lie unclaimed, and unused.

We need to know, what we, as spiritual beings, have become in Christ, so that we can bring the other two aspects of our being, namely our bodies and souls, into alignment with our spotless spirits. We do this by renewing our minds and presenting our bodies as living sacrifices.

Our spirits are 100% pure and always in perfect tune with God. We are a new species of being that never existed before. At the precise moment of our transformation, we were immediately capable of all kinds of supernatural exploits, such as raising the dead, casting out demons, healing the sick and all manner of miraculous feats.

Our spirit man can commune with God and enjoy an intimate relationship with Him. We can participate in the joy of God, the love of God, the peace of God and so much more. All of these possibilities are within us, yet most Christians don't recognize it, and consequently don't benefit from it. How sad!

Although they may acknowledge that God lives within them, they pray as though he doesn't. We often hear prayers that invite Him to "come" to them to meet their needs, as though He is not already within them. It would seem that they have not grasped the concept that God merged Himself with them at the precise moment of their rebirth—redefining them as *"new creatures"*. His presence within us empowers us to do the works of Jesus. He is not a distant god somewhere in the cosmos. The power to heal the sick, raise the dead, set those who are in bondage free, resides within us in the person of His Holy Spirit.

When we got born-again, our spirits were totally transformed into something very different to what we were. In an instant our spirits become as perfect and as pure as they will be in heaven. You could say that one third of our salvation was accomplished, not needing any further improvement—immune from any and all contamination from sin—not requiring cleansing or recharging. What we are right now in spirit, we will be for all time and eternity!

For the rest of our lives, we are to renew our minds to accept who we are and what we have in Christ. Our bodies and actions need to be brought into alignment with our new spirit identity. Our spirits are completely saved, and no amount of law keeping can make our salvation any surer.

"As He is, so are we in this world" (1 John 4:17b NKJV). On the inside, we do not have to become like Jesus—according to this verse, we are already like Him. We have everything we will ever need on the inside. That leaves us with the responsibility of getting our minds and our bodies to fall into line with what has taken place within. But unless we know who we are in Christ, it's simply not going to happen. We are to educate ourselves to the point where we are thoroughly convinced that we are completely new and distinctly different to our previous identity.

We are body, soul and spirit. Our bodies aren't necessarily evil; they are just in the physical or natural realm. Our spirits are always in tune with God—they have His life, His divine nature and His holy character.

Our souls (i.e. minds) must decide, either to take their cue from our spirits, or from the five senses of our bodies. If we allow our five senses to call the shots, we will continue to be subjected to the dominance of the physical realm. A simple majority of two against one—our bodies and souls ganging up against our spirits. That's all it takes to undermine our spiritual authority.

If the doctor says that we will die, and we believe it, it is a simple majority. When our minds have sided with the pain in our bodies, our spirits are simply outvoted. We may have the life of God within us with enough power to heal us, but healing will not manifest if we are more sensitive to our bodies and their demands, than to our spirits and their provisions.

If on the other hand, we get our minds into agreement with our spirits, it is a simple majority of two against one—our bodies are outvoted and therefore can be healed. That's when our souls (i.e. our minds) draw healing and health from our spirits.

Our spirits always have the power of God to heal. When our thinking comes into agreement with our spirits, we connect to God's provisions within us. Peace, healing, deliverance, power to raise the dead etc., are contained in our spirits, ready and waiting for us to appropriate in Jesus' name.

Much of the Christian world agrees that God can heal, but in reality, few live in divine health and/or experience miraculous healings. They know that He can do these wonderful things, but believe that they have to seek Him, and then beg and plead with Him. They may even go so far as to get as many people as possible to pray for them, as though God needs to be persuaded, overwhelmed by sheer force of numbers, before reluctantly conceding to come through for them. But if our spirits are already identical to Jesus' Spirit, we are complete in every sense of the word; having the very same virtue that raised Jesus from the dead residing within us.

We don't need Jesus to "come" and give us something—He, together with everything He could possibly give us, is already within us. Perfect peace, perfect joy, perfect health, perfect provisions and perfect faith have already been deposited within our spirits. It's not a matter of God having to bring us something else; it's a matter of understanding what we already have and learning how to release it.

If we don't get this right, we end up misdirecting our prayers. The prayer of authority is simple—it's a matter of speaking health to sickness; provisions to lack; peace to turmoil, and so on. All of this can be drawn from what we already have within us. We even have authority to speak these blessings in Jesus' name, thus speaking on His behalf.

When the willingness of the Healer is in question, prayers falter. But once convinced of His willingness, faith takes on a sense of confidence. No longer dealing with ifs and buts; dealing with indisputable certainties! Once we are entirely convinced that we are fully empowered to perform miracles; not in any way dependent on a third party's whims and fancies (not that God has whims and fancies), our prayers take on an air of confidence. There is no need to conjure up some kind of imploring faith to persuade somebody somewhere out there to perform a miracle for us. If we don't know what is contained within us, we won't know what can be withdrawn from within us.

"Acknowledging of every good thing which is in you in Christ Jesus" (Philemon 1:6). We are to acknowledge that every good thing deposited within us is more than able to deal with every eventuality in life. Clearly, there is no need to beg and plead for something that is already in our possession. Faith is so much more effective when we are convinced of what we possess. Once convinced, the need for begging comes to a decisive end. Rather than wondering whether or not God will concede to our requests, we simply dispense His virtues with unshakable confidence!

Our prayers cannot be effective if we are expecting something from the wrong source. God decided to place the source of His power within us. He chose to partner with us, thus turning us into divinely composite beings—His Spirit combined with ours. Once combined, He granted us authority to dispense His power from within.

Quite obviously, even though we have permission to use His power, for as long as we don't acknowledge having this privilege, it remains unused. Only those who are convinced that they have the authority to use it, will use it. What a crying shame! Believers are not supposed to be victims of circumstance; circumstances are supposed to be victims of believers!

No longer should we approach our problems as mere human beings. We are no longer mere human beings; we are wall-to-wall Holy Ghost. If we dare to acknowledge what we possess, the supernatural will become second nature—opening the way to enormous possibilities!

We are not just old sinners saved by grace. We are a whole new species of being that has never existed before. *"Therefore if any man be in Christ, he is a new creature: old things are passed away; behold, all things are become new"* (2Cor 5:17 KJV).

We need to look at the spiritual mirror, not to see how poorly we shape up, but to see who we are and what we have in Christ. *"(God) has blessed us with all spiritual blessings"* (Eph 1:3 NKJV). We need to come into agreement with what the Word of God says about us.

We are a spirit, we have a soul and we live in a body. Our bodies are merely earth-suits. Astronauts wear spacesuits. Clearly, the spacesuit is not the person living inside it. Similarly, a person's body is not the person living inside it.

Just as a spacesuit enables people to live in the hostile environment of space, so our earth-suits enable us to live in the earth's environment. Just as the spacesuit only goes where the person wearing it desires, so our bodies should be controlled by the desires of our spirits. In other words, if our spirits contain healing power, then we should not allow our bodies to call the shots. Our spirits should be calling the shots and telling sickness where to go!

It takes words spoken in faith to appropriate healing, forcing sickness to leave. It is for us to choose to believe for wholeness, and to declare it into existence. But if we do, we had better be prepared for a tantrum—our bodies will scream out for attention, demanding that we speak "feelings" rather than "faith".

Sickness is in bodies, whereas health is in our spirits. Now it is up to our minds to choose either to bow to the sickness contained in our bodies, or to the health and healing contained in our spirits. Either we buckle under the pressure of symptoms, or we take charge of them, declaring emphatic words of healing and health. When faith is spoken, healing is more real to us than the pain we feel. Our faith is the bridge we use to cross over into the miraculous!

"And that ye put on the new man, which after God is created in righteousness and true holiness" (Eph 4:24 KJV). When we were born-again, we were instantly recreated, brand new individuals, entirely righteous and pristinely holy—a matter of inner transformation! Now it is up to us to shift inner transformation into outward living.

Right now, we are as righteous as we will ever be. By trying to become more righteous, we succeed only in becoming more self-righteous, and God cannot be approached on the basis of self-righteousness. *"God is Spirit and those that worship Him must worship Him in spirit and in truth"*. (John 4:24KJV).

Self-righteousness stands on self-performance. Problem is, no-one's performance is reliable enough to reach divine righteousness. To rely upon our performance, is to rely upon inconsistency, which in turn results in inconsistent faith—sometimes up and sometimes down, thus ineffective. On the other hand, if we are relying upon the righteous state of our spirits, we are relying upon something that is infinitely consistent—always completely righteous, always completely holy!

"As He is, so are we in this world". (1 John 4:17 KJV) This being the case, why don't we always feel that we are like Him? It's because we

have allowed physical realities to dictate. But if we allow the Spirit to rule, this is what happens: *"But when the Holy Spirit controls our lives, he will produce this kind of fruit in us: love, joy, peace, patience, kindness, goodness, faithfulness, gentleness, and self-control"* (Gal 5:22,23 NLT).

In the spirit we are always brimming over with love, joy, peace, longsuffering, kindness, goodness, faithfulness, gentleness and self-control. We are one and the same spirit, identical to Jesus. *"But the person who is joined to the Lord becomes one spirit with him"* (1 Cor 6:17 NLT). We don't always reflect this in our behaviour, but that doesn't change our "oneness" with Him. For as long as we allow our bodies to call the shots, our behaviour is going to let us down, but when we allow our spirits to have the last say, the Spirit of God is able to produce His fruit—He will never let us down.

If the Spirit of God can never be sinful or depressed, and we are one spirit with Him, then it follows that our spirits can never be sinful or depressed. Yes, our minds can be depressed, but not our spirits—they are mirror images of Jesus. Sadly, when we allow our bodies to call the shots, we become victims of mood swings, never quite sure of our authority.

Although we contain enough power to change our circumstances, sadly, the power we have is seldom activated. Obviously, for as long as we are not convinced that we have it, we won't make use of it. But if our conclusions are based on the promises rather than on the circumstances, then, with declarations of faith, we can bring circumstances into subjection to the promises.

The key is to give more credibility to who we are in Christ than to who we are in our circumstances! We need never despair—knowing that physical conditions are subject to our God given authority—as we release God's favour through words of faith, contrary circumstances must submit!

Once convinced of what we have, we can appropriate what we have. But for as long as we don't know what we have, it follows that we won't know what can be appropriated. We can die of thirst, even while sitting on a hidden water well in the desert. But once we are aware of it, we can draw water from it and survive. Similarly, for as long as we don't know what we contain, we cannot appropriate what we contain. Someone may have deposited a small fortune into our bank account. But for as long as we don't know about it, we could live as paupers. Sadly, this is a perfect analogy of the great majority of believers!

We can do greater works than Jesus did. *"The truth is, anyone who believes in me will do the same works I have done, and even greater works, because I am going to be with the Father"* (John 14:12 NLT). Later He commanded us to do these works.

"Such as I have, give I thee, in the name of Jesus of Nazareth rise up and walk" (Acts 3:6 KJV). Here is the model prayer for the sick. Peter didn't pray for God to heal the man, he simply told the man to get up on the strength of what Peter had. He said, *"Such as I have give I thee"*. He didn't say, "such as God has give I thee". Inside of us is precisely the same Spirit that was in Peter.

Two thousand years ago, Jesus said, *"It is finished"*, and He really meant what He said. In one fell swoop, the stripes He took on His back took care of all future healings—He would never have to perform another healing. From His side, healing is a fait accompli! Then He placed His Spirit, which includes His healing power, within each of us. Now the responsibility for healing no longer rests with God; it rests with us. It is still His power, but it no longer depends on Him as to whether or not we get healed. It depends entirely on whether or not we draw healing from our spirits—our spirits are divinely merged with His. We activate the process with words of faith—commanding sicknesses to go in the name of Jesus. If we don't acknowledge that we already have this life-giving power at our disposal, we are likely to waste our breaths, asking God for stuff He has already given us.

If after giving you my watch, you were to continue pleading for me to give it to you, I would not be able to give it to you a second time—it is already in your possession. If you continue pleading, I would have to conclude that you are losing your mind. In the same way, you already possess the power to heal and perform miracles—it's within you—there is no reason to continue asking for it—there is nothing more to be given.

God has already borne our sicknesses and placed this virtue within us. He doesn't have to go back to the whipping post to obtain more healing. *"Freely you have received, freely give"* (Mat 10:8 KJV). God cannot violate what he has said. He said, *"You heal the sick".* We should be out there doing what He told us to do—healing the sick, raising the dead and casting out demons. His words are not suggestions; they are commands! May I ask—have we been obedient to His commands? Have we been raising the dead? If we claim to be obedient, then surely we would not hesitate to get on with it!

Of course, we cannot do this if we don't know what God has deposited within us; neither can we do it if we deny that we have it. God has placed the same power inside of us that was inside Jesus. *"The eyes of your understanding being enlightened; that you may know what is the hope of His calling, what are the riches of the glory of His inheritance in the saints, and what is the exceeding greatness of His power toward us who believe, according to the working of His mighty power which He worked in Christ when*

He raised Him from the dead and seated Him at His right hand in the heavenly places" (Eph 1:18-20 NKJV).

In this prayer, Paul didn't pray for God to give us something; he prayed for God to reveal something to us—he wanted us to grasp the concept of possessing the same spirit that raised Jesus from the dead. More than that, he prayed that we would discover our divine identities—we are *"in Christ"*—in the god-class of being. In coming to terms with our true identities, we come to terms with the enormity of the power residing within us.

We may think that if we can just plead enough, or get enough people to agree with us, we will be able to twist God's arm, or wear Him down with tiresome begging—as though He needs to be persuaded to do something good. Sadly, that's the approach of religion. On the other hand, the approach of a follower of Jesus is, "Thank you Lord for depositing the miraculous within me. Show me how to draw from it. I believe—help my unbelief". It's an entirely different approach. One way operates with uncertainty, while the other, with unshakable confidence! One way with pitiful pleading, while the other, with unflinching boldness!

The greatest manifestation of the power of God was demonstrated in the raising of Jesus from the dead. The same "raising the dead" kind of power resides within us. Paul prayed, "show them", not give it to them.

We don't have a power problem; we have a knowledge problem. We perish for a lack of knowledge—ignorant of who we are *"in Christ"*. We tend to see everything from a physical and human standpoint. We tend to relate to God by what we are in the physical realm, not realising that God must be approached through spirit and truth. In this way, we don't only miss out on His miraculous power; we also miss out on divine intimacy and the peace that passes all understanding—it's a package deal!

Some think that faith is a matter of denying reality. This is wrong. You are not trying to make something real that isn't real. You are simply drawing reality from your spirit and transferring it to the physical. Before the physical universe was created, only the spiritual existed.

"By faith we understand that the worlds were framed by the word of God, so that the things which are seen were not made of things which are visible" (Heb 11:3 NKJV). The physical worlds were created by faith. Faith takes what already exists in the spiritual and manifests it in the physical. Some might say, "If I can't see it, it doesn't exist". But if we are living purely by our five senses, we are no better off than animals. Animals only have their five senses to go by.

Wherever you are right now, you are surrounded by uncountable TV signals traveling through the air. The fact that you can't see them doesn't mean that they don't exist. In the same way that these signals need to be taken from the unseen realm into the seen realm by turning a TV set on, we are to transfer the unseen provisions from the spiritual realm to the physical realm by turning our faith on. In doing so, we tap into what is already within us. It is not a matter of pleading with God to do something; it's a matter of using what He provided some two thousand years ago.

Those who come to embrace this concept, cease to wrestle with uncertainty. It is no longer the age-old question: "We know that God is able, but how can we be sure that He is willing?" This is not a question in the minds of those who know their covenant rights. Their faith takes on an air of confidence—based on irrefutable certainty.

Faith teaching got a bad rap from people who completely misunderstood the concept of calling *"those things that be not as though they were"* (Rom 4:17 KJV). They labelled them the "name it, claim it, frame it freaks". How unfortunate for the critics—their words simply reveal their ignorance—they don't know about the power within them. Sadly, in denying the existence of their empowerment, they reduce their divine effectiveness to nothing more than human feebleness.

We are not to deny that things exist; we are to deny their "right" to exist. In as much as it is true that we are sick; it is also true that all the healing we desire exists within our spirits, the divine part of us. The fact that it can't be seen, doesn't mean that it doesn't exist. Though unseen, it is every bit as real as anything that can be seen. It is simply a matter of moving reality from the unseen realm into the seen realm. It awaits our instructions!

Often people assume that if the pain leaves, then God has decided to heal them, and if it stays, He has decided not to heal them. This misunderstanding arises when we are of the opinion that it is God's decision to heal or not heal. Little do they know that God has already decided. Some two thousand years ago, He provided all the healing He is ever going to provide. Then by His sovereign will, He deposited this completed work within us, authorising us to move it from the invisible realm to the visible realm. It is easier to deliver something already in our possession, than to deliver something that might or might not be sent to us.

When it came to healing, how did Peter speak with such confidence and authority? The answer is that he knew what he possessed and therefore knew what he could give away!

Elisha's servant was overwhelmed when he saw that they were outnumbered by the enemy surrounding them. So Elisha said, *"Fear not: for they that be with us are more than they that be with them"* (2 Kings 6:16). Then Elisha prayed that his servant's eyes would be opened to see into the unseen realm. Immediately his servant saw that the mountain was full of horses and chariots of fire.

His servant was the only one to see into the spiritual realm—not even Elisha saw it. Elisha was working purely by faith; not by sight. He believed despite not seeing. Given the choice, of either working by faith or working by sight, most people would choose sight—a very limiting choice. Faith carries so much more authority and resources than what can be seen.

Most believers would put more credibility in a fatal medical report, than in what God has to say on a matter. If the Doctor says they have cancer, and the word of God says that by His stripes they were healed, they would tend to lend more credence to the doctor's report. The question is: Whose report will you believe?

Surely, we should not give more credence to reports that disagree with God, than to reports that agree with Him. For a believer, God's reports are as credible as credibility gets! Faith does not deal in unrealities; no, it deals with reality at a much higher level. The spiritual is not unreality; it is every bit as real as the physical, only infinitely superior. Always bear in mind, the first report is not the final report.

We don't have to withhold our rejoicing until we see the materialisation of a miracle. The moment we have declared our faith on a matter, our confidence is proof in itself—no need to wait and see. That's because ownership takes place at the point of declaration; not at the point of manifestation.

Faith looks past physical reality into the spiritual realm, and what it conceives, it declares, thus shifting unseen reality into physical reality. The door into the realm of the spirit is imagination. We are to imagine our way into the future that God has already provided. Imagination opens the door for faith to be the conduit to convey God's provisions from the spiritual realm into the natural realm. Clearly, the only reason that we do not boldly declare things into existence, is because we are not entirely convinced that we actually possess the authority to do so.

We are to live by faith; not just visit faith when backed into a corner. Also, living by faith is not just for those in ministry who must make ends meet without the benefit of a regular salary. It's meant to be the normal way of life for all believers.

The spiritual realm is more credible than the physical—it is the very source of life. Tragically, by and large, the administration of the supernatural has been left in the hands of the clergy. How sad—the supernatural should be second nature to every believer—an everyday way of life!

About forty years ago, I went through seemingly endless bouts of flu, barely recovering from one bout, before being put out of action by another. Neither medicine nor prayer were making the faintest difference. To top it all, my absence from business was having a seriously detrimental effect on my ability to support my family.

In sheer desperation, I came across a book by Charles Capps on the power of the tongue. Encouraged by its message, I committed to quoting scriptures concerning healing—repeatedly confessing that I would not receive a cold or flu. Whenever I sneezed, I would simply state, "I do not receive a cold, flu or virus in Jesus' name". What was the result, you may ask? I have not had a single bout of cold or flu in almost forty years. After such a long defeat, Satan knows where he stands with me on this issue. In the last forty years, I have not taken a single day's sick leave. Praise God!

We process God's promises by speaking them into existence by faith. How long is the process? One minute? One month? One year? If we are prepared to process it for as long as it takes, it will happen. Conversely, we empower our fears by speaking them. In as much as words give substance to promises, they give substance to fears.

"But without faith it is impossible to please Him, for he who comes to God must believe that He is, and that He is a rewarder of those who diligently seek Him" (Heb 11:6 KJV).

The good news is: God doesn't just tolerate us, He likes us. Not only does He like us; He is deeply in love with us! He is pleased with us! He sees something quite different in us to what we see in ourselves. *"Therefore, if anyone is in Christ, he is a new creation; old things have passed away; behold, all things have become new"* (2 Cor 5:17 NKJV). We are not in the process of changing into new creatures, we are already new creatures. *"But you are not in the flesh but in the Spirit, if indeed the Spirit of God dwells in you. Now if anyone does not have the Spirit of Christ, he is not His"* (Rom 8:9 NKJV). We have His Spirit in us. *"That which is born of the flesh is flesh, and that which is born of the Spirit is spirit"* (John 3:6 NKJV). We are no longer sinners. The old sinful beings that we once were, were crucified with Christ—they no longer exist. Now that we are born of the Spirit, we are every bit as sinless as Jesus in God's sight.

"But he who is joined to the Lord is one spirit with Him" (1 Cor 6:17 NKJV). We are one and the same spirit as Jesus—ounce for ounce, identical in every respect. Identical in His love, identical in His power, identical in His joy—this is what it means to be one spirit with Him. If He isn't depressed, afraid or sick, then neither are we depressed,

afraid or sick. Our Christian life is a process of discovering who we are in the spirit, and then transferring this discovery to the physical realm.

"For as he thinks in his heart, so is he" (Prov 23:7 NKJV). Unfortunately, we do not always think right thoughts about who we are, and this results in us living less significant lives. If we dare to accept that we have the same anointing Jesus had on earth, we will live in high victory, and do even greater works than He did. The same One who opened deaf ears, blind eyes and raised the dead, lives inside us. But we cannot do what Jesus did unless we acknowledge that we are as He is. *"As He is, so are we in this world"* (1Jn 4:17 NKJV).

If it hasn't been working for us, it is probably because we haven't perceived how enormously empowered we are. It all revolves around our thinking. Right thinking doesn't come naturally; it takes dedicated commitment to meditate and speak in line with God's words. It takes an unwavering commitment to convince our minds of the gravity of His presence within us. Correct focus is called for. How sad to live a whole lifetime without coming to terms with the enormity of the divinity bestowed upon us.

We have been given every reason to expect more than what is humanly possible—we are fully empowered to override physical impossibilities with supernatural possibilities! No matter how great we think the power of God within us is, it is always greater—we are simply not capable of comprehending the enormity of it. Deny this if you will. Just bear in mind that we can only release as much power as we believe we have. It all hinges on knowing who we are in Christ. Identity is everything—fundamental to victorious living!

Fortunately, sin does not penetrate through into our spirits. Our spirits are vacuum-packed holiness. Although outwardly, we may not always be what we would want to be, our spirits are always what we would want to be.

If we believe that we are not welcome in His presence when there is sin in our lives, then we have bought Satan's lie, and He will eat our lunch and pop our lunch bags. Yes, people deal with us on the basis of our performance, but not God.

"Not with the blood of goats and calves, but with His own blood He entered the Most Holy Place once for all, having obtained eternal redemption" (Heb 9:12 NKJV). It took only one entry into the Most Holy Place to obtain our eternal redemption. And Jesus did it for us. By the way that some believers pray, one would think that Jesus obtained "temporary" redemption, and that it lapses every time they sin. This is not so—we retain our righteous standing despite our sin.

In that case, should we yield to sin? *"Do you not know that to whom you present yourselves slaves to obey, you are that one's slaves whom you obey?"* (Rom 6:16 NKJV). Give Satan half a chance and he will make a meal of us with depression and all kinds of harmful ills.

The first portion of this chapter was inspired by Andrew Womack's "The Gospel Truth" TV Programme.

Sinless

"Those who have been born into God's family do not sin, because God's life is in them. So they can't keep on sinning, because they have been born of God" (1 John 3:9 NLT). Note that this scripture doesn't say that we must not sin, although that goes without saying; it says we cannot sin—in other words we are incapable of sinning. In light of the obvious state of our many moral failings and weaknesses, how should we understand

this scripture? If the general state of conduct within the church and its leadership is anything to go by, then it would seem that no-one is saved! Or perchance, could we have misunderstood this scripture?

In the same letter, John goes on to make it clear that Christians do sin. *"If we say we have no sin, we are only fooling ourselves and refusing to accept the truth"* (1 John 1:8 NLT). Just in case we didn't get it the first time, he reiterates: *"If we claim we have not sinned, we are calling God a liar and showing that his word has no place in our hearts"* (1 John 1:10 NLT). If we still didn't get it, he goes on to say: *"My dear children, I am writing this to you so that you will not sin. But if you do sin, there is someone to plead for you before the Father. He is Jesus Christ, the one who pleases God completely"* (1 John 2:1 NLT). So there is no doubt that John was patently aware that we as Christians do sin.

So what's up John? First you say Christians don't sin, and then you say they do. Sounds awfully contradictory! Either he got it wrong, or we got it wrong. Clearly, the Word of God would be unreliable if it contradicted itself. We know with absolute certainty that God's Word is entirely reliable, so we must look a little closer to see how these apparent contradictions harmonise.

We are body, soul and spirit. When we look at the three parts of man as having different connections, the puzzle suddenly falls into place, and makes perfectly good sense. We are a spirit, we have a mind and we live in a body. Our bodies are made from dust and connected to this earth. Our spirits are made from incorruptible seed and connected to God. Our minds are either influenced by the natural, being our five senses, or by the divine, being our godlike spirits.

The only aspect of your being that got reborn was your spirit. It was instantly recreated into an entirely new creature that had no previous existence—absolutely sinless—incapable of committing sin all the way into eternity. Your body, on the other hand, was not recreated—the warts on your hands before rebirth, are still there after rebirth. The same goes for your mind—you are still capable of the same nasty thoughts after rebirth.

Our recreated spirits are exactly as pure and sinless as Jesus', and that's why we have direct access into His presence to worship and petition. It is also the reason that we will be ushered straight into heaven when we leave this planet one day. If it were in any way possible for our spirits to be corrupted, we would not have this access—after all, God cannot look upon sin, regretfully, something we all do.

Old Testament saints did not have this privilege—none of them were born-again. After their deaths, they were kept in a waiting place called Paradise, looking forward to the day when Jesus would redeem them. He would validate their animal sacrifices with Himself as the final sacrifice. Before the cross, the High Priest could only enter the holy of holies with the blood of animals.

Because we were born of incorruptible seed, our spirits are incorruptible. This allows us to enter His presence boldly any day of the week (1Pet 1:23). Sin takes place in our souls, not our sinless spirits. That's why we are always the righteousness of God in Christ, regardless of our yet to be conquered sin.

If we can truly embrace the thought that our spirits are every bit as pure as God's, we will gain a new level of confidence to declare His promises with emphatic assurance. Basing our favour with God upon how well we have performed, is an exercise in futility. How can we ever be sure that our performance is hitting the mark? In light of such uncertainty, how could anyone possibly be convinced that their prayers will be answered?

Will the knowledge of such generosity cause us to abuse our privileges? If it does, it simply shows that we haven't got a clue of what grace is all about. The fact that some misguided believers have distorted the meaning of grace to allow them to indulge in sin, should not give us reason to be suspicious of grace.

We are not reckoned to be the righteousness of God in Christ by reason of not sinning. We are dead to sin, not dead to sinning. Our day to day sins, however terrible, don't cancel our position of right-standing with God. Our righteousness was not awarded to us for not sinning, and therefore cannot be withdrawn from us for sinning.

We do not strive to become righteous. That's not how right standing is achieved. The one and only way to have righteousness is to have it graciously conferred upon us—something that took place at rebirth. Our day to day practical sanctification takes place as we allow the Holy Spirit to guide us. Under His control, our actions are the actions of Jesus. Yet many would deny this and consequently are left to fruitlessly strive to be like Him.

Those who strive for righteousness through sheer grit and determination, obtain nothing more than "filthy rags". But when you know that you are already 100% righteous, you can relax. You know that you already possess what religious people so desperately strive for. You rest in the finished work of the cross, and seemingly as if by accident, discover that you are slowly but surely losing your appetite for sin. Then it is just a matter of allowing the life changing process of sanctification to quietly run its life changing course.

Human nature finds it difficult to surrender to accusers, but has no problem surrendering to those who love them, especially if love comes without conditions. Thankfully, this is the kind of love God gives!

The good news is that God relates to us as though we have never put a foot wrong. How wonderful to know that our divine relationship is based upon His love and righteousness; not ours!

SUBTLE INFILTRATION

Control—The Spirit of Jezebel

The good news of the Gospel is in its "liberation". Churches are divided into two distinct categories. Some surreptitiously use the fear of deathly consequences to enforce their ideas of holiness, while others use grace to entice believers into holiness.

Controlling churches are usually not aware that they have strayed from the grace of the gospel. Their denominational version of grace seems perfectly right to them, and nobody can convince them otherwise. They could not imagine being any freer than they already are. To them, more freedom would lead to more sin.

How do we know whether a Church is pastor controlled or Spirit led? Some churches may say that they are not legalistic and therefore not pastor controlled. A church may be relaxed on such issues as fashion, make-up, dancing, drinking and the like, but it is not this that distinguishes them as liberated.

A church is controlling if the pastor tells his people how to live, using the wrath of God to frighten them into holiness. Conversely, a church is liberated if the pastor connects his people to the Holy Spirit and leaves them in His hands, allowing Him to lead as He wills.

Pastors are not commissioned to "scare" congregants into holiness; they are commissioned to "connect" congregants to the Holy Spirit. There is enough good news to draw people into repenting—God's love and favour are persuasive enough. *"The goodness of God leads you to repentance"* (Rom 2:4 NKJV)

How can we know whether we are wrath motivated or love motivated?

Wrath Motivated	Love Motivated
• Commanded to stay away from sin.	• Lose appetite for sin.
• Kept from sinning by the fear of God.	• Kept from sinning by the love of God.
• Strive to stay out of sin.	• Take no pleasure in sin.
• Strive for God's love.	• Rest in God's love.
• Grit our teeth to love unlovable people.	• Loving unlovable people comes naturally.
• Love because we are commanded to do so.	• Love because we are loved.
• Strive for approval.	• Rest in Jesus.
• Guilt leads to feelings of unworthiness.	• Acquittal leads to feelings of value.
• Conditional love engenders self-doubt.	• Unconditional love engenders self-worth.
• Easily tempted—the flesh is weak.	• Not easily tempted—the Spirit is strong.

- Measure our value by our performance.
- Uncertainty in prayer.
- Repent from sin.
- Motivated by fear.

- Measure our value by God's love.
- Confidence in prayer.
- Repent "towards" God.
- Motivated by love.

Of course, nobody would purposely choose guilt and condemnation, yet so many innocently open the door to it through law keeping. All it can achieve is uncertainty in prayer! For law keepers, there is always this unanswerable question at the back of their minds: "Have I scored sufficient points to get my prayers answered?"

The road called grace is paved with the Father's love, mercy and undeserved favour. For some odd reason we have come to prefer beating ourselves half to death for the very blunders that Jesus took a beating for on our behalf. He did this in order to remove guilt and condemnation from the equation. Sadly, many are more conscious of their guilt than of their right-standing.

Human nature is drawn in the direction of its predominant focus. The law, being sin focused, cannot perpetuate righteousness; it can only perpetuate what it is focused upon, i.e. sin. Thankfully, the reverse also applies. Those who are conscious of their imputed righteousness are drawn into righteous living!

If you are going to switch to grace, it has to be all or nothing at all. (Matthew 13:44 NKJV) *"Again, the kingdom of heaven is like treasure hidden in a field, which a man found and hid; and for joy over it he goes and sells all that he has and buys that field"*. You can purchase the field called grace, but the price is very dear. The cost is: no more condemnation, no more guilt, no more feelings of unworthiness, no more pressure to change. Costly, isn't it? You're right—it's a freebee! And we cannot afford to miss it!

Sadly, for many sincere believers, Sundays have become disinheritance days. If we are taught that grace is conditional, the conditions will distance us from grace. When the message of *"the law of sin and death"* is preached, inheritances are forfeited, and God's grace and favour, cancelled (Gal 5:4 NLT).

Satan's strategy is to keep believers' inheritances out of reach. He will do anything to distance them from the favour God planned for them. If he can get us to replace grace with good honest religious striving, he has won the day. If he can convince the clergy that it is their responsibility to keep their flocks out of sin, their flocks won't look to the Holy Spirit for true sanctification.

When congregants fall into serious sin, the clergy may feel duty bound to reinforce moral fences, and to tighten up on moral policing. Seeing that their flocks consist of voluntary members, the screws cannot be applied by withhold pay cheques, but that doesn't leave them powerless—fear can be used to scare people into obedience. It can be pretty scary when Old Testament curses are misused to manipulate.

Let's be honest, there is no pleasure in attending disinheritance Sunday services. Believers go to these meetings out of religious duty, rather than out of eagerness. Beware, fear has only one reward, and it is not holiness, it's just another form of bondage—the very opposite to the freedom that Jesus obtained for us at great personal cost.

Fearful hellfire and brimstone preaching may frighten us away from sin, but sadly, enslave us into performing for favours. Followers will do anything to appease an angry god. Sadly, without the help of a loving Father, we are left to conquer strongholds with sheer grit and determination.

On the other hand, when connected to an empathetic Father, we are drawn into a loving relationship. He doesn't judge; He goes out of His way to love His children, regardless of whether they are nasty or nice. He wants them to find personal value for themselves in His love—enough value to give them reason to cease looking for value in all the wrong places. When this happens, Godly lifestyles follow without effort.

In using fear to motivate morality, churchgoers become enslaved to performance; a bondage every bit as oppressive as the bondage from which they were saved.

How is it possible to love a Father who is angry with us? Thankfully, He is not! He doesn't want a cowering relationship. In as much as He loves us, He desires to be loved. A fearful relationship of cowering is more akin to slavery than to family. When we must love, simply because it is expected of us, is it really love at all? For love to be genuine, it must be a "want to", not a "have to".

Fortunately, God is not annoyed with us; He is in love with us. Not being confined to time and space, He has already seen all our future betrayals, duplicities, vices and iniquities, yet loves us all the same!

I have heard of people who have had face-to-face encounters with Jesus in recent times. None of them speak of His judgement—there is not even a hint of accusation in His eyes. It's as though His absolute acceptance of them, despite their many failings, is immensely overpowering—they can hardly stand the intensity of His love!

Coming face to face with graciousness of this magnitude is irresistible—non-judgemental love and acceptance is immensely influential! The goodness of God is too awesome to ignore. When His love draws us closer, resistance melts and defences drop. His love brings the very best out of us—repentance follows with eagerness!

It is the goodness of God that leads us to repentance (Rom 2:4).

Notice that this verse does not say that repentance leads to the goodness of God. That would be putting the cart before the horse. We have had this one back to front for so long, that we tend not to take God's sequence seriously. To understand the sequence, is to understand grace—get it wrong, and become a slave to religious performance! God's goodness and grace comes before repentance; not after! We do not repent to gain His goodness. By its very nature, grace must be undeserved—it is not granted to the deserving.

Preachers who hold out a carrot, offering God's goodness as a reward for repentance, are making empty promises. It doesn't work that way! It is the knowledge and experience of His pure "agape" love, with no strings attached, that leads to heart felt repentance. It takes nothing less than His agape love to change us.

Repentance towards God is key! It is how we transfer responsibility to Him. Surely, it must be obvious! God would never expect us to strive for something that cannot be attained. We have not been invited to enter His gym to get nowhere on a treadmill; we have been invited to enter His rest. It is time to relax—fall into His loving embrace, and trust Him to do what He promised!

When fear is used to motivate us to be more loving, we are likely to contrive a pseudo form of love. Better not to love at all than to sham love—there is enough flakiness doing the rounds without adding to it. Let's face it, shallowness eventually wears thin and is ultimately exposed for what it is. When that happens, friendships come under pressure.

We used to sing a beautiful chorus, "I love you with the love of the Lord". How wonderful! Unfortunately, many of those singing this lovely song were simply passing the buck. Ultimately, the reality of the depth of their love came out. When put under strain, relationships fell apart.

Ever heard the Christianese saying, "I can't stand so and so, but as a Christian I must love him, so I will just have to love him by faith". Can anything be more empty than that? If you were at the receiving end of such shallowness, how loved would you feel? Imagine if God was that insincere with us. People are crying out for authenticity—how sad to give them superficiality.

In ancient Greek and Roman times, actors would double up on stage roles, using different face masks for different roles. This kind of acting was known as "hupokritēs" from which we derive the English word "hypocrites". The actor behind the mask, contrived a personality for the part he was portraying.

If we love people simply because we are told to, we too are hypocrites. Imagine two Christians who can't stand each other telling each other that they love each other in the Lord. This is hypocrisy at its best. No wonder the world sees Christians as hypocrites. We must concede—more often than not, they are correct.

This is not the brand of love that Jesus had in mind when He commanded us to love one another. We are apt to give it when deserved; He gives it regardless. Our love is often shallow and fragile; His is not. He is well aware of our many weaknesses and short comings and does not fall out of love with us because of them. Of course, although mankind cannot produce this degree of love, we do have the privilege of allowing Him to display the fruit of His Spirit through us.

His chief fruit is genuine love. As much as He wishes to show His love to the world, He cannot do it, except through willing conduits. For that, He requires yielded hearts. Let's face it, nothing is more influential than love and acceptance, especially when we are only too aware that we have done absolutely nothing to deserve such honour.

Before we say that we love others, let us at least have the courtesy to love them regardless of their duplicities and betrayals. If they are too repulsive to love, we can draw love from the well of God's love within us. When we love as He does, lives are touched in special ways! It is easy to love somebody who deserves to be loved, but there is a special kind of joy in giving and receiving love for no good reason at all! Such love is heart-warming, not only for the receiver, but also for the giver!

Christianity is not meant to be about giving love under duress; it's about loved hearts overflowing with God's love.

There is a day coming when our works will be judged and rewarded. On that day, there will be no rewards for works done with reciprocation in mind. Conversely, works conveyed with nothing but love in mind, will be well rewarded! It takes outright graciousness to make a difference to the world around us!

If you instructed your child to brush his teeth and to tell you that he loves you, you would have nothing of which to rejoice when he dutifully goes through the required routine. On the other hand, if he were to spontaneously throw his arms around your neck and whisper in your ear, "I love you daddy", you would have good reason to rejoice! In the same way, God is longing to receive genuine love and worship from us. He couldn't possibly be moved by worship given just because it must be given, nor is He moved when it is given by force of habit.

Once we have tasted God's love, there is no further need to be driven into holiness—no need for legalism to bully us into it. Isn't it wonderful? Our love is shaped by His goodness; not by His wrath. While being divinely romanced, to our surprise, we notice that we are not acting and reacting as we once did!

Religion honestly believes that, without the restraints of the law, we will fall headlong into sin. But what religion just doesn't seem to get, is that fear motivation plays directly into Satan's hands. When we do good simply to avoid the consequences of not doing good, we are living in fear; the very thing that debilitates faith! Once debilitated, we have no further access to God's favour. For as long as we insist on striving for godliness, we forfeit godliness. The law can only reveal ungodliness; it does not possess the power to confer godliness.

Satan just stands by rubbing his hands in glee as he watches guilt and unworthiness take good honest believers out at the knees. He doesn't have to lift a finger—He just looks on as self-loathing and despondency do his work for him—like taking candy from a baby. For many, the joy of the Lord is a distant dream that is sung about on Sundays, but seldom experienced in day to day living.

God has specifically removed judgement and fear from the equation. No matter how well orated, condemnatory sermons contribute nothing but shame, putting God's favour beyond the reach of sincere believers.

"Until the law sin was in the world, but sin is not imputed when there is no law". (Rom 5:13 KJV). Although sin was in the world during the period between Adam and Moses, this scripture makes it clear that sin was not imputed or credited to anybody during that period. By the same token, since the cross, sin is not imputed or credited to New Covenant believers—the law no longer has jurisdiction over them. *"God was in Christ reconciling the world to Himself, not imputing their transgressions to them"* (2Cor 5:19a KJV). Paul says that sin cannot be imputed when there is no law, and fortunately, Old Covenant law no longer applies to New Covenant believers. Sin is simply not counted against us, in the same way that it was not counted against anybody who lived before the time of Moses.

The first murder was committed by Cain when he killed his brother Abel. This took place many years before the establishment of the Ten Commandments. How did God deal with such a diabolical crime? If the law had been applicable at that time, God would have required Cain's life in exchange for Abel's. As it turned out, God did not require Cain's life, rather he protected him. (Gen 4:15).

Contrast this with the first crime committed after the law had been instituted. It was the serious crime of collecting firewood on a Sabbath day. Would you agree that collecting sticks is less heinous than murder? Under the law, the penalty for picking up sticks on the Sabbath was death. Imagine that! He had to be put to death for choosing the wrong day of the week to collect firewood for his family.

Many still insist that we must keep the law. It is difficult to understand why they would choose harsh penalties and dreadful curses. Fortunately, in the present dispensation, we are no longer under the law, so we can expect God to treat our sin in a similar way to Cain's. A hard pill for Pharisaic Christians to swallow.

In attempting to gain God's favour through law keeping, we put ourselves under a curse. *"For as many as are of the works of the law are under the curse; for it is written, "Cursed is everyone who does not continue in all things which are written in the book of the law, to do them""* (Gal 3:10 KJV). How do we explain the rationale of religion? How do we explain why anybody would choose a life of curse dodging? Jesus has a better way. His way is called grace!

You cannot say that you do most of the law and therefore are okay. Nine tenths of the law does not give you nine tenths blessings and one tenth curses. No! You get ten tenths of the curses for failing to fulfil one tiny part of the law. With so many warnings in scripture, why would anybody purposely go out of their way to invite curses upon themselves? The law is a minefield—don't go there!

New Testament believers get the blessings of Deuteronomy 28, not for fulfilling the law, but for believing—it is by faith alone! If we were expected to gain the blessings by doing all of the law, then the blessings would forever be unattainable. Our best performance simply cannot meet with the required standard. All we would get for our trouble would be the awful curses listed in the same chapter.

Clearly, God cannot be approached by virtue of our works; He can only be approached by virtue of the Blood Covenant.

In my early Christian years, I always felt that I needed to confess all my sins just in case I died in an accident. Whenever boarding an aeroplane, I would make sure that I was up to date with my confessions. My conviction was that, if I were to die, I would not go to heaven—unconfessed sin would have kept me out.

This was a crazy notion. If there was any truth to it, then only those who died while busy confessing would be saved. There is always a time lag between sinning and repenting. Nobody repents of a sin at the precise moment of committing the sin, thus leaving an un-repented gap. The question is: Are we unsaved during these gaps? The good news is, God does not impute or credit any sin to our accounts. (Rom 5:13). Our slate remains clean, even though, as much as we would not want to sin, we continue to be tempted and don't always choose well.

Jesus did not just die for our pre-conversion sins; He died for all sins, from Adam to eternity. This does not mean that we should not repent; it just means that from God's side, He does not attribute sins to our account.

All the same, repentance is no less important. When we regard sin in our hearts, shame disables our faith. Nonetheless, *"There is no judgement awaiting those who trust Him"* (John 3:18 NLT). Did you notice that this exemption is for trusting and not for holiness?

One of South Africa's foremost church leaders was seemingly enjoying great success, planting new churches both here and abroad. All his churches were thriving; some to the point of overflowing. His preaching was particularly strong on holiness and morality. He came down especially hard on adultery, preaching hellfire and damnation on infidelity. He would call on unmarried young adults and teens to publicly pledge an oath; vowing sexual purity. Thereafter, he would pronounce an Old Testament curse upon those who would dare to break their vow.

Instead of keeping them from sexual sin, he succeeded only in stirring their passions for one another, putting many of them into deep guilt and condemnation. The church dealt with this by applying public discipline, public repentance and on-going counselling.

One Sunday he proclaimed from his pulpit that he had told God to strike him dead with lightning if he ever committed adultery.

I had opportunity to speak to him about his radical statement. I shared my understanding of God's gracious ways—how He uses love to change us; not fear of being struck by lightning. I reminded him that many moralistic preachers taking the same hard line, had ended up falling on the very issues they had so ardently preached against. He was adamant that this could never happen to him.

He strongly disagreed with me on the issue of grace, sighting a grace movement called the "Invisible Church". He said that they became completely invisible when they disappeared like a vapour.

He told me that my view was too radical for his liking. He insisted on holiness by the fear of God, and slated what he called "greasy grace". He insisted on disciplining members who would dare to step out of line.

He often put people on the spot when they came forward for prayer. He would ask them to confess their sins before a packed congregation. Unfortunately, the more discipline he meted out, the more infidelity mushroomed in his congregation. Sadly, his demand for holiness resulted in the precise opposite.

Then just as he was riding the crest of the wave, the unthinkable happened. He fell into the very same sin that he had so vehemently opposed. He had been having an affair with one of his associate lady pastors. Fortunately, in discrediting himself, he discredited a religious fallacy that claims that holiness can be achieved without the aid of grace. And so ended an influential ministry. Though he taught holiness and demanded it of his congregation, ultimately, when push came to shove, his brand of holiness proved to be hollow!

Some may blame these misfortunes on inadequate moral control. But beefing up moral control doesn't solve the problem; it exacerbates the problem! This pastor's controlling ways were the very reason for sin plaguing his congregation. Controls and rules don't restrain sin; they incite sin! Yes, visible behaviour may be temporarily restrained, but core problems seated in hearts remain untouched—it takes love of the agape kind to make a real difference! How do we explain: Although grace is the one and only answer to the sin predicament, it is often viewed with scepticism.

Holiness by self-effort is godless, and therein lies the problem. Unless God Himself is the one who sanctifies, He is not party to our "holiness". Is there any wonder that so many flounder? When God is missing from the process, our attempts at holiness are nothing more than window dressing, and that's why God calls it *"filthy rags"*.

It should be a relief for the clergy to know that it is not their responsibility to change people. God has a plan to do this all by Himself—He does it by way of His Holy Spirit. Once people have been connected to the Holy Spirit, there is only one thing left to do, and that is to obey His promptings without hesitation.

So often, the yoke that preachers place upon the shoulders of their flocks is so burdensome that not even the preachers themselves are able to bear them, often buckling under the weight of their own moral demands. The ministry is strewn with casualties of the advocates of morality, who have fallen on the very same issues they so passionately denounce. Satan sets them up with laws that cannot be kept, and then quietly waits for them to take themselves out.

But doesn't God punish us? No, not at all! Hard times are for our education; not for our punishment. He wants us to receive His best, so hard times become opportunities for Him to mould us into vessels fit to contain His gracious favour.

God is not a killjoy. He is not trying to take good things from us; He is trying to get good things to us, using tough times to get our attention. Our inadequacies give us reason to turn to Him—He is more than adequate!

God has done all He can to give us access to our inheritances. As much as He desires to favour us without requiring any payment, we insist on trying to prove our worthiness. But our best shot at worthy making just doesn't cut it with God. We forget that Jesus has already made us entirely worthy!

Sometimes, it takes hitting rock bottom before turning to God. But when we do, a door opens for us to step into a life of privilege and favour. Often our foundations need to be knocked out from under us, so that stronger ones can be constructed in their place—robust enough to carry an enormously blessed life.

Whatever we focus on, we make room for. Focus on trying to avoid immorality and reap immorality. Focus on the goodness of God and reap His goodness.

God said that everything produces after its kind. Churches are factories that produce one of two kinds of products. Pharisee factories produce performers, while grace factories produce people of faith. Mix faith with law and end up with Pharisees—people who pride themselves on living up to the church's expectations. Sadly, it is offence taking and judgementalism that makes Christianity distasteful to the world. Besides, self-achieved piety does not impress God—to Him it's nothing but smelly rags!

MASS DISINHERITANCE

In the late 1970's, our small church building could seat one hundred and fifty people, but our average attendance was less than fifty. One of our members got a vision to build a new sanctuary in the suburbs that would seat three hundred and fifty. Some of our members did not approve of such extravagance, especially in view of our long history of low church attendance. Despite their objections, we went ahead with the project in the hope that it would ultimately attract a higher attendance.

Then came the official opening. We held our breath in anticipation of a good turnout. To our surprise, the church was full, albeit with the help of invited guests and dignitaries. We were overjoyed, but the true test was yet to come. How many would attend our first regular Sunday service? That was the day our hearts sank. There were only about fifty—manly the old faithfuls. For the next few months we saw no growth in numbers.

Then something quite remarkable happened. Almost overnight the church was full to capacity. Where previously, the congregation consisted mainly of three-generation families, suddenly the congregation consisted almost entirely of youth. What really surprised us, was that these young converts were immediately ablaze for God. Their fervour and spiritual hunger took us by surprise—the Christianity of long-standing members seemed dull by comparison. By and large, these new converts came to us without any church background. But instead of being a handicap, it proved to be a distinct advantage. They came into an unencumbered relationship with God, without the help, or more correctly, the burden of legalism and church traditions.

Clearly, we were witnessing a move of the Spirit. The zeal of these young converts outshone the dreary religion of longstanding members. Years of religiousness had lulled us into a sense of complacency—we had become comfortable with unspectacular Christianity.

To our surprise, these new believers had found favour with God without the help of the legalism that we had so dutifully observed. The magnitude of what we were witnessing was way beyond the wildest stretch of our imagination!

At first, this freedom was of concern to the elders. But they soon came to realise that their cherished brand of religion was dry by comparison. These youngsters were firebrands! We had to admit that the rule keeping we had thought important, had served only to impede our Christianity.

To the credit of the stalwarts, the Holy Spirit was given room to move. To the extent that we were able to break free from legalism, we discovered new liberty in God's grace. These new Christians had an innocent naivety about them—they only knew about grace—their wings had not been clipped by legalism.

Like sponges, they soaked up all the Bible teaching they could get.

They would spontaneously pitch up at church on their skateboards and bicycles during school holidays, just in case there was any teaching or praise and worship on the go. Our youth pastor had his time cut out trying to satisfy their insatiable thirst for things spiritual. Frivolous youth church fun and games were of no interest to them.

The revival spread to a junior school. When a teacher left her classroom, a twelve-year-old newly born-again girl, took the opportunity to witness to her class. She led each and every one of them in the sinner's prayer, immediately followed by baptism in the Holy Ghost. After school, she marched them off to her home, where she personally baptised each and every one of them in her bathtub.

Long standing Christians were being prayed for by these youngsters. They would fall under the power of the Spirit and get up healed, delivered and set free.

Soon the new church was too small. On Sunday evenings, you could not find a seat, even if you arrived half an hour early. Despite additional seating down the aisles, in front of the pulpit, on the stage and foyer, people were being turned away at the door long before service started. The ushers did their best to accommodate as many as possible, seating youngsters on any open floor space, even underneath the grand piano.

With the church filled to capacity long before services started, our pianist would attempt to play background music. But background music was impossible. As soon as the congregation recognised the tune, they would spontaneously join in, singing with gusto. Half an hour later, at official starting time, the worship team band would strike up. No need for them to create an atmosphere of worship; the congregation was already enraptured with Jesus!

We, the older members, had to rethink what we considered to be proper. We could not deny that, despite their unreligiousness, the experiences of these young radicals were genuine—to them the supernatural was normal. With a measure of trepidation, the elders allowed it to blossom. As it developed, it became more and more apparent that we were witnessing a mighty move of God!

Obviously, *"where the spirit of the Lord is, there is liberty"* (2Cor 3:17 KJV). But liberty can seem scary to religious folk. Although we, the older folk, had moved towards liberty, we were not entirely comfortable with it. We thought that we had moved far enough, but unbeknown to us, our former religious legacies continued to hamper us—preventing us from sharing in their level of liberation in Jesus.

Unfortunately, about five years into the awakening, the revival came to an abrupt end. This happened after one of the elders described the revival as a runaway freight train without brakes. Leadership felt that they had extended too much room for the development of grace for comfort.

The liberties that accompanied freedom scared leadership. They concluded that it wasn't enough for these youngsters to be spiritually savvy; they needed moral instruction. And so, a measure of legalism was reintroduced. With legalism came control. But what the elders did not understand was that control is the mortal enemy of grace, and opposites cancel each other! Sadly, this is all it took to extinguish a once glorious spiritual awakening!

Not even the appointment of a new Pastor could stem the steady decline from spiritual vibrancy to religious mundaneness—from grace to legalism.

Later, the elders introduced a document titled, "The Spiritual and Moral Qualifications for Church Membership". This was a desperate attempt to force congregants to bow to legalism. The document listed the moral qualifications and lifestyle requirements for continued membership of the church. Each and every member was required to pledge their commitment to the code by signing a copy of the document.

Sadly, in reducing the liberty of the Spirit to nothing more than a moral code, they had empowered legalism to triumph over grace! We had gone full circle, from the restrictiveness of legalism, to the liberty of grace, followed by a return to the same religious drudgery. Sadly, this is all it took to smother the last smouldering embers of a once raging fire of an authentic move of God. With this, the revival was finally and permanently snuffed out.

Sadly, this church never recovered—its empty pews and financial woes continue to testify to the catastrophic failure of church control. Once a beacon of light, beaming God's loving grace to the city, this church now stands as a hollow monument to "grace defeated"! As tragic as it is, it serves as a reminder that we dare not reduce the essence of the gospel to a moral code.

All Christians instantly receive full entitlement to their inheritances at the precise moment of rebirth. Seeing that we all start our Christian journey supernaturally empowered, why are so many of us failing to walk in the supernatural? How did devil beaters turn into dreary church goers—up at times and down at times? The answer is simply that they have been disinherited by a list of do's and don'ts. This tragic story is not unique—it mirrors much of the modern day church.

What begins in the unforced rhythms of grace, ends up in the trashcan of do's and don'ts. Some converts are robbed immediately after rebirth, and others a little later. Sincere leaders are blissfully unaware that rule setting serves only to disinherit sincere followers. Sadly, they themselves were disinherited in the very same way. So, they came to terms with less, settling for a sub-level of victory, resigning themselves to believe that what they are experiencing is as much as God intended for them to experience. It doesn't bother them that they are not raising the dead as a matter of routine.

Contrary to what Jesus predicted, they have come to accept that they have never done greater works than Jesus and are most unlikely to do so in the future (Joh 14:12). They have rationalised unanswered prayers to are due to, "Not having prayed in line with God's will"; "Not being in God's timing"; "Not having sufficient faith"; "Not having the right motives"; "Praying for our greed instead of our need"; "Likened it to Paul's thorn in the flesh" or "God cannot answer our prayers if we are not living in purity". They may not be aware that the reason for unanswered prayer, could be due to a sense of unworthiness and shame, due to failing to live up to their church's expectations. This mind-set is faith debilitating and favour destroying—its only reward is disinheritance!

Although nobody in the history of mankind has ever managed to achieve a completely pure lifestyle, it is nevertheless God's desire that we continuously move towards purity in a practical sense. But this should not be seen as a means of qualifying to be favoured by God. This could not have been illustrated more clearly than in Jesus' ministry. Never once did He turn a single person away for their less than godly living. We cannot assume that everyone who asked Him for healing was living in pristine purity, yet He healed them regardless. He required their faith, not their holiness—never once making an issue of their lack of holiness before administering healing.

The Centurion, being non-Jewish, did not keep the law, yet Jesus commended his faith, saying that it was superior to the faith of Jewish law-keepers. He received his miracle without first having to change his pagan beliefs or mend his ungodly lifestyle. Never once did Jesus so much as hint that a person cannot be healed before repenting.

There are only two recordings of Him telling anybody not to sin. One of them was to the woman who was caught in adultery. But He only mentioned this after reassuring her that He did not condemn her. This incident had nothing to do with sin getting in the way of prayer. Her prayer had already been answered when her accusers walked away. Only after she received her miracle, did He make any mention of her sin, and even then, He assured her that He was not standing in condemnation of her.

The simplicity of enjoying God's plan to favour us can so easily be wrecked by the thought that we won't be favoured unless we get our lives in order.

LOVE WITHOUT REASON

The enormity of divine generosity cannot be grasped by mortals. Humanity is easily offended; divine love is not! It stretches far enough to love murderers while in the very act of murdering the Saviour of the world. Instead of condemning them, Jesus asked His Father to forgive them, and then, as their unsolicited advocate, made a case for their pardon, bringing mitigating circumstances to His Father's notice— telling Him that they were acting in ignorance. In His words, *"Father forgive them for they do not know what they are doing"*.

I have heard a lot said about how far love stretches, but this degree of sacrificial love takes the cake! Can any normal person's forgiveness really stretch that far? On occasion, I have been known to cut slack, but only to a point. My limited sense of tolerance doesn't come close to God's seriously radical measure of love—to my limited thinking, it borders on irrationality!

God is the employer who paid a full day's wage to everybody He employed, regardless of how many hours they worked that day. What kind of love would give a full day's wage to someone who was only employed for a few minutes? It doesn't make economic sense.

In the parable of the prodigal son, He is the Father who refuses to take his self-righteous elder son's advice to shun his delinquent son. Before the prodigal managed to utter a single word of his well-rehearsed apology for his inexcusable behaviour, his father had him in his embrace. Instead of chiding him, he put a robe over his filthy body, a ring on his finger, sandals on his feet and called for a celebration.

This is the son who had dragged the family name through the mud. Surely, he deserved to be hauled over the coals for the irreparable damage he had brought upon the family name—to say nothing of the family fortune he had so wantonly squandered! Where are his father's words of outrage? Doesn't he know that such generous love and grace could be mistaken for weakness?

Jesus was the friend of sinners, prostitutes, drunkards and crooks, and was not embarrassed for snobbish religious society to know it. Doesn't He know that religious people will find such associations distasteful, even scandalous? What kind of love compelled him to risk his reputation like this? Society finds such associations offensive. To me it is sheer madness—playing directly into the hands of His critics. What kind of love does that?

In his book "Lion and Lamb", Brennan Manning states: God's love is based on nothing, and the fact that it is based on nothing makes us secure. Were it based on anything we do, and that "anything" were to collapse, then God's love would crumble as well. But with the God of Jesus, no such thing could possibly happen. People who realise this can live freely and to the full.

Remember Atlas, who carries the whole world? We have Christian Atlases who mistakenly carry the burden of trying to deserve God's love. Even the mere watching of their strivings is depressing. I'd like to say to Atlas: "Put the globe down and dance on it. That's why God made it." And to those weary Christian Atlases: "Lay down your load and build your life on God's love." We don't have to earn God's love, neither do we have to repay it. It is a free gift. Jesus calls out: "Come to Me, all you Atlases who are weary and find life burdensome, and I will refresh you".

The unmerited love of God can be disturbing. The idea of reward without work, might put a break on our dedication to the Gospel. I mean, why struggle to do good if God loves so recklessly and foolishly? It appears to be a valid question.

But those who truly know the God of Jesus are not likely to ask why they should be labouring for the kingdom while others stand around all day idle. They want life and they have found the fullness of life in God Himself. The rest of us may ask why we should bother to live uprightly if God is going to be so generous, but not those who have found the God of Jesus.

The love of God embodied in Jesus is radically different from our natural way of loving. As a man, I am drawn to love appealing things and persons. I am attracted by certain qualities that I find congenial. When I love as a man, I am drawn by the good perceived in the other. I love someone for what I find in him or her.

Our Heavenly Father is very different. He loves us, not for what He discovers in us, but for what He is in Himself. He doesn't love us because He has found something in us worthy of admiration, nor does He only love good people. It is because He is so incredibly good that He loves everybody, whether good or bad. He even loves those who are incapable of giving or receiving love, the miserable, the utterly unlovable. He does not search for the convivial, appealing, comely, to respond to with favour. The fact is, He never responds—He always initiates love. Love begins with Him seemingly without reason.

Jesus lives for those in whom love is non-existent. In dying that His killers may live, He reveals to us a Father that is without wrath. Our Father cannot be offended or impressed with what we do or don't do. The Lord does not treat us as we deserve—if that were the case, we would be desolate—but He treats us as dearly loved children—He is unable to do otherwise. What this says is that our heavenly Father is gracious. His love is abounding in extent, defying our wildest imaginations.

Knowing that we are deeply and sincerely liked by someone produces a tenderness in us. If I sense that you truly like me, not in the way that you may feel that you must love me as a brother in Christ, you cause me to experience a new level of self-respect, self-esteem and wholesome self-love. By accepting me exactly as I am, my fears are banished. My defences—sarcasm, aloofness, name-dropping, self-righteousness, boasting, giving the appearance of having it all together—melt away. I become secure enough to drop my mask of pretence. You infuse self-confidence in me, allowing me to expose my weaknesses and shortcomings without fearing your scorn. The look in your eyes permits me to take a journey into my inner-self, there to make peace with that part of me that was unable to experience peace. I soften, become more open, sincere, vulnerable, and affectionate—dropping my defences and respond with equal warmth.

Do you sincerely believe that God personally likes you as an individual—not loves you because He promised to and therefore has to? What is your answer? God loves you by nature, He does not have to make an exception for your behaviour whether good or bad. He is genuinely very fond of you and this knowledge should cause you to experience a relaxed state of serenity, to the point where you can have compassion on yourself; automatically reflecting His tenderness towards all of those with whom you interact. God says: "Does a woman forget her baby at the breast, or fail to cherish the son of her womb? Yet if these forget, I will never forget you" (Isaiah 49:15 JB).

Go for it. How wildly can you hope, how crazy can you dream, how big can you imagine that God loves you? At the point where your hopes, dreams and imagination end, the love of your heavenly Father only begins. Because *"eye hath not seen, nor the ear heard, neither have entered into the heart of man, the things which God hath prepared for them that love Him"* (1 Cor 2:9, KJV).

Once again, the question arises: Will the awareness that God loves us regardless, lead us into spiritual slothfulness and moral laxity? On the surface, this seems to be a rational fear, but in reality, the exact opposite is true. I know that Susan loves me just as I am and not as I ought to be. Do you think that her love for me is an invitation for me to be unfaithful to her and become reckless with our marriage? On the contrary—love invites love. Now with absolute freedom I am able to respond to her love. Similarly, the deeper our roots sink into the love of God, the more generously we are able to love in return.

This kind of love enables us to find love and acceptance for ourselves. We are enabled to love ourselves just as we are, because we are convinced that this is the way that we are loved by God. Our spiritual growth no longer concerns us; it takes care of itself. By understanding our desirability to our Father, we are able to dispose of the oppressive standards and demands that we impose upon ourselves, and release ourselves from the pressure of "must do" and "ought to do".

To some extent it is true to say that each of us arrive at our own conclusions about who God is, and our conclusions become our image of Him. Seeing that there are so many diverse opinions, it is quite feasible that we have settled upon wrong conclusions. It is also true that the particular image that we have formed of Him determines the value that we see in ourselves. The distortion that we believe of Him, becomes the distortion that we will believe of ourselves. Afterall, we can only hope to become more like the God that we have come to imagine Him to be. Knowing the love of our heavenly Father, results in a more compassionate attitude towards ourselves. Our heavenly Father's love fosters our love. In healing the personal image we have of our Father, we heal the personal image that we have of ourselves.

The reason for Christ's Incarnation was to show us the faithful love of our Father: "The reason I was born, the reason why I came into this world, is to testify of the truth." The truth is the reliability of God's love. *"We saw His glory, the glory that is His as the only Son of the Father, full of grace and truth"* (John 1:14, JB). In healing our image of God, we heal our image of ourselves.

The old religious image of a vindictive and mean God gives way in Jesus to the God of love who cherishes us and has made His abode within us. Jesus revealed a God who does not demand but gives; does not oppress but lifts up; does not hurt but heals. A God who forgives when we deserve condemnation, and liberates when we deserve punishment. Woe to those who demand, control, oppress, judge, wound, condemn, and punish their flock in His name. Obviously, they do not truly know Him.

Do we truly know Him? Maybe we have given more priority to other things in our Christian walks, than to knowing Him; thanking Him; praising Him; worshipping Him; submitting to Him; living by the golden rule etc. The many things that make up Christian living are all rooted in knowing God and discovering His love.

Perhaps we may think that, because we read the Bible, we know a great deal about God. This is far from true. What good does it do us to know chapter and verse if we have not begun to understand and experience the extent of His love for us.

Though we are Christians, we can be so busy with Christian duties that we don't have time to patiently wait to hear God's voice from within. Just allowing God to love us, is more import than prayer. *"Be still and know that I am God"* (Psalm 46:10 KJV).

Luxuriating in His love can be somewhat like sunbathing. People notice that we have been in the sun—our tan, a sure give away. Basking in the sunshine of God's love makes us look different. Knowing that we are loved causes us to sparkle from within without trying. There is a ready smile and a spring to our step that we didn't put there. We have a gracious response towards every ungracious action done to us. This is because we have the confidence that comes from knowing that we are unconditionally loved by somebody who really matters to us. Soak up every last ray. You'll glow from the inside!

CONCLUSION

We have two seemingly opposing views—the message of divine reward, and the message of divine grace. The message of reward sets out to achieve holiness in order to find acceptance with the Father, while the message of grace reveals that we are accepted and every bit as righteous as Jesus from the moment of our rebirths.

In the message of reward, the level of our holiness determines the level of our relationship with God. Whereas in the message of grace, our relationship is measured by His righteousness; not ours! Our responsibility is to believe and rest in this truth. The message of reward demands that we strive to modify our behaviour, but grace teaches that, in yielding to God's love, our hearts are changed, resulting in unforced godly behaviour.

Bob lived a reasonably good life, always trying to live by the Golden Rule: "Do unto others what you would have them do unto you". He felt he was doing well enough without any need to go to church. Afterall, to him, Christians were hypocrites. They didn't swear, smoke or drink, but they wouldn't hesitate to stab their best friends in the back for the sake of gaining an advantage. He thought that, based on his standard, which he felt was higher than the standard displayed by the Christians he knew, he would easily make it to heaven.

Then one day, Bob heard that Jesus had said that anger made him guilty of breaking the sixth commandment—thou shalt not kill. And that looking lustfully upon a woman made him guilty of breaking the seventh commandment—thou shalt not commit adultery. For the first time, the truth dawned on him; he was not going to make heaven by his merits. He wasn't a bad person, but something as insignificant as his private thought life had disqualified him. Clearly, self-righteousness was not enough. Thus began his search for a way out.

Then he was told that God had made a way for him to escape his sorry condition. God had already put the blame for all his sins on His son, Jesus. Consequently, right standing with God could be his for the asking.

He could hardly believe his good fortune—with Jesus he could still make it. He decided to ask God to forgive him for his sins and asked Jesus to be Lord of His life. This was a new beginning for Bob. He was still suspicious of church people, so didn't attend church at first. He thought that reading his Bible was enough. With the help of a trusted friend, he discovered that all of his sins were completely washed away, and that he now had a loving Father with whom he could share his life's dreams.

During this time, his friend showed him from the word that he was no longer a sinner—blameless before God. In fact, in Christ he was as righteous as God. His friend was careful not to make a fuss of his many sins—he left that task to the Holy Spirit. He urged him to always listen to the Holy Spirit, and to do whatever the Spirit told him to do.

Convinced of his new blameless identity in Christ, he discovered that he could ask God for anything and everything. He thrived on the supernatural, experiencing miracles on a regular basis. He found that God was interested in the most insignificant details of life, like providing convenient parking bays with time on the meters. Despite his many failings, He flourished in the warmth of God's companionship. With God's help, he felt invincible!

He would obey the still small voice within—eagerly submitting to the Spirit's promptings. No sooner did he celebrate the victory over one sin, than another would be revealed to him. Without hesitation, he would repent towards God. Habits that he couldn't overcome were effortlessly resolved without the slightest hint of striving on his part— God's love was changing Him from within.

Then he sensed the Holy Spirit prompting him to fellowship with other believers. So, he obediently started going to church. He enjoyed mixing with other believers, but soon discovered that they were content with less remarkable living than he was experiencing. For them, the supernatural was rare. They seemed to speak a lot about triumphant living, but the way things turned out for them, seemed to contradict their boast. He was determined not to allow himself to become as spiritually ineffective. It perplexed him to understand how such devout church goers could be content with such mediocrity.

Then came a sermon on unclean vessels. According to the Preacher, God could not use a vessel that was unclean and tainted with sin. Sounded right; but then came a list of sins that could taint one's vessel. To his surprise, he was guilty of almost all of them. For the first time, he saw himself in a different light. Instead of the innocent blood washed pure sinless new creature that he had thought he was, he discovered that he was a miserable sinner, unfit for the Master's use. That day he left church burdened with a sense of shame.

He was informed that his holiness could be reinstated with repentance, and that if he proved to be faithful, he could regain his right to enter the throne room of God with boldness as before.

It was not only his innocence that he lost that day, God seemed distant to him, and his prayers, ineffective. He thought he was doing everything the church required of him, but there were no more convenient parking bays. Gone were moments of sweet fellowship with his Lord—instead, intimidated by His presence. At the back of his mind was this nagging thought that he may have offended God.

Something had changed. But it wasn't God—He never changes. What could it be then? The shocking truth of the matter is that the very religion he had come to cherish, was the religion that had disinherited him.

But the Pastor assured him that there was hope for him—he just had to try a bit harder. So, he immediately embarked upon a quest to modify his behaviour. Instead of the Holy Spirit gently guiding him with one task at a time, the church threw the kitchen sink at him. He had a whole heap of straightening out to do—enough to drown him in self-despisement and unworthiness.

Although overwhelmed, he welcomed any opportunity to restore his relationship with God—desperately wanting to regain the intimacy he once knew and cherished. But the problem was that he was making and breaking new resolutions far too often for his liking, causing him to feel ever more guilty. To top it all, still more rules were being offloaded on him to help him fulfil the rules he was failing to fulfil.

This did not deter him—he was prepared to do whatever it took—so desperate was he to be right with God. Sadly, more rules meant more un-kept rules. The task was beyond him. Ultimately, Bob resigned himself to the fact that he was not able to change himself.

Feeling helpless and alone—his earlier victorious days, now a distant memory. He questioned himself, "Were those days really all that good, or was it just a figment of my imagination?"

With the passage of time, he learnt to hide his shortcomings, putting up a reasonably acceptable front. The task of masking his flaws became easier with practice. After a time, no-one suspected that he had a problem with anger, at least not until his best friend betrayed him. That was the day he lost his cool and told him where to get off in no uncertain terms. He used words that he thought he had victory over. They seemed to jump out of his mouth from nowhere. Unfortunately for him, his embarrassing outburst was witnessed by a church Elder.

Next Sunday the message from the pulpit was on anger with some reference made to bad language. How embarrassing! The shame of it added to his unworthiness. In addition, he felt betrayed—the trusted Elder had obviously informed the Pastor. This led to another confrontation, this time with the Elder, and unfortunately, he let his temper get the better of him. The Elder took the matter up with the Pastor. Next the church board decided to discipline him. He was asked to step down from all public duties until such time as he showed fruit of repentance. The embarrassment was almost too much to bear. Now all he wanted was out—what was he to do? Church wasn't fun anymore!

Then his Pastor went to some special meetings in another town and returned with a completely new outlook. He told the congregation that he had unwittingly misled them by giving them the wrong picture of their heavenly Father's character. God was good and wasn't angry with them! He had put his sinless Spirit in each and every born-again believer, making them one with Himself. They were completely perfect in Christ, and although they could not stand in their own righteousness, they could stand in His. The good news was that none of their sins would ever be credited to them.

They could approach the throne of grace with boldness to find help in time of need. No need to mend their ways to gain His favour. There was covenant and a free inheritance that they could draw from as and when they wished. Although they did not have to clean up their acts, he urged them to be obedient to the leading of the Holy Spirit—ready to obey His every prompting. Their new understanding of God's love would give them personal value. And healthy self-esteem would transform their actions.

Bob was feeling so low that he found it difficult to believe that it could be that easy. Surely God would require more of him. His pastor patiently guided him—slowly but surely convincing him that God expected nothing from him but faith, and a readiness to respond to the Holy Spirit's gentle promptings.

With time he regained the joy of sweet fellowship with his heavenly Father. More than that, he soon discovered that he was no longer doing the stuff that had gotten him into so much trouble. God's love was slowly but surely transforming him from within.

Bob's story is not unique. As with a parable, I hope you get the point. Every day, people are losing their innocence, and forfeiting their inheritances. God is saying to you, forget everything that you have ever heard about Jesus, if it doesn't begin and end with love!

God has so much more for us than a set of rules that make us look good. I believe that if we can grasp these simple concepts, we will experience victory over the flesh as never before. They position us on a guiltless launching pad from which our faith can skyrocket to new heights. With the bright light of God's love in our lives, the Bible comes alive and takes on new meaning—victorious living soon follows in an unforced way. Only when we abandon all striving, and relax in the finished work of the cross, do we enter the rest that Jesus promised we would have.

Grace Misunderstood

If after reading this book, you have come to conclude that grace is all well and good, but God cannot look on sin, and therefore the onus is on us to live holy, then you have missed the point of grace by a country mile. The whole point about grace is that it empowers us to overcome sin effortlessly. Let's be honest—our most diligent striving has made us look good, but done little to change us inwardly. All this time, God had a better way for us than our feeble and ineffective strivings. His way really works—it is grace!

"Everything that does not come from faith is sin" (Rom 14:23 NIV). Wow! What a difficult concept to come to terms with! Why would normal everyday living be sin? Simply put: Everything achieved by faith in God, is achieved by His wisdom and power, not ours, and therefore not sin. And whatever is achieved through faith is achieved by grace! Clearly, self-effort to holiness is not of faith, and therefore, as good as our intensions may be, God sees it for what it is— *"filthy rags"*!

Visualise yourself standing before the Father. If you are dressed in your personal holiness, you are dressed in filthy rags. But once we have admitted to our sinfulness, and turned to Jesus for His righteousness, we are clad in the pure white garments of His holiness; not ours. D.I.Y. Holiness is not in the least bit holy—nobody could possibly feel comfortable standing before God clothed in the filthy rags of their flimsy efforts to be holy.

The righteousness of God conferred upon us remains pristinely pure—entirely unblemished by our sins. But our day to day behaviour needs time to adjust to the righteous person we are in Christ. Clearly, religion's idea of holiness is not God's idea of holiness—it falls horribly short of His immaculate standard. Unless change takes place at heart level, it is not holiness—not even close! It takes an understanding of the depth of His love to bring about inward change. Loved hearts are yielded hearts—transforming behaviour without effort!

There is a man that I truly admire. He is the most selfless person I know. He cared for his aging parents and aging mother-in-law, always including their needs in his plans, no matter the cost. Every house he owned has had to have special accommodation for his parents. His two lovely children are serving the Lord. He was often involved in fund raising for his church. He planted and nurtured a new church among the underprivileged. He is guileless and gracious, always considerate and caring. All who have had the privilege of knowing him, cannot help but admire him. I hold him in the highest regard and could go on singing his praises. One day I asked him if his righteousness could be compared to Jesus'. His answer was, "Of course not!"

If our best efforts and highest standards are substandard by God's measure, then we have all missed the mark. The law leaves us in no doubt whatsoever—God's standard is nothing short of perfection! Seeing that no amount of self-effort can ever attain perfection, how can we possibly attain it? The choice is simple: Either we strive to attain it by flawed self-effort, or we rest in God's flawless grace and allow His Holy Spirit to guide us. I trust you have made the right call!

"For whoever keeps the whole law and yet stumbles at just one point is guilty of breaking all of it" (Jam 2:10 NIV).

"For if you are trying to make yourselves right with God by keeping the law, you have been cut off from Christ! You have fallen away from God's grace" (Gal 5:4 NLT). Serious stuff, wouldn't you say?

Mars is seventy-eight million kilometres from the earth at its nearest point in its orbit. If a rocket, aiming to reach Mars, were only one degree off course when leaving the earth, it would miss Mars by hundreds of thousands of kilometres. If we were to add one law to grace, we would only be a tiny degree off course, but a tiny degree is all it takes to miss our inheritances altogether. Like the rocket, we end up lost in the deep darkness of disinheritance, hundreds of thousands of kilometres from grace—a life of marvellous favour forfeited for the sake of fitting in. Tragically, much of the church has cautioned sincere seekers to be suspicious of any notion of grace being extreme. Sadly, in buying into this distortion, they forego so much of God's favour!

What must you do to receive your inheritance? Relax—cease from striving—you are loved! Your inheritance is ready for collection. The executor, appointed by Jesus to wind up His vast estate, must carry out His wishes as clearly specified in His Last Will and Testament. You, as one of the named beneficiaries, have every right to lay claim to assets bequeathed to you. He is waiting to hear from you right now. What is your instruction? He stands by, ready to honour all demands made against the assets of heaven—they are jointly owned by you and Jesus! He asks only that your instructions be validated. All it takes to validate your claim is the application of faith together with the password. The password is the name of our Lord Jesus. Whatever you fail to withdraw will be held in your trust account, available to be withdrawn whenever desired. Don't leave your assets lying idle—put them to good use!

The Father's love for you is undying! You are free to indulge in His affection—He is besotted with you! Go ahead—make His day—fall into His loving embrace. You will never be the same again!

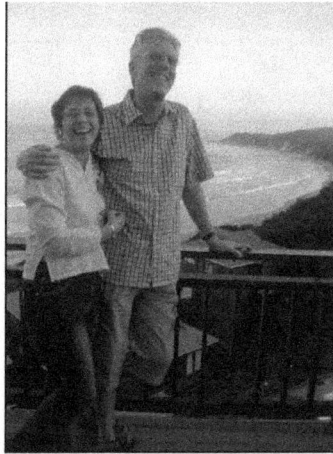

Deon and Susan

Also by this author:

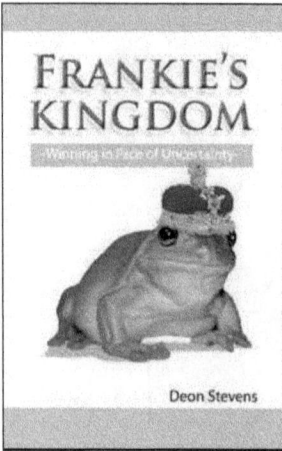

I believe that Deon is a strategic champion of a Glorious Grace revolution taking place throughout the earth. This is not a book of empty froth, bubbles and shadows but it has the substance of rich unveiled truth unfolding in a supernatural sequence of liberating revelation that will set your heart racing with joy and inspire a fresh love for Jesus. All things are possible to a people set free from uncertainty, confusion and condemnation. Thank you so much Deon for your courage and compassion. I honour you and salute you in His abundant Grace.

Rob Rufus, Pastor of City Church International Hong Kong.

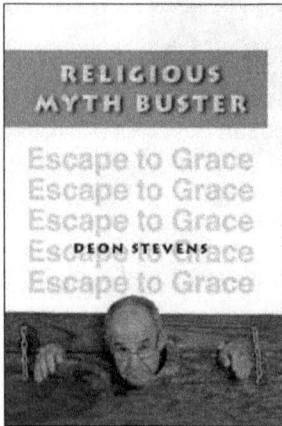

How is it that eager new believers turn into dreary religious zombies? What is the process that destroys a new believer's free spirit?

Babes in Christ soon lose their individuality as they are pressed into the mould of religious conformity. Religion is a killer! If religion was a man, he ought to be strung up from the nearest tree.

What is the solution? Realising that we are loved in our present condition, without having to make any promises to change, is the greatest discovery that any believer can make. God would rather relate to weird and wonderful misfits, oddballs and characters, than to a whole army of terracotta soldiers. God's unconditional love gives us freedom to be ourselves. It is okay to live with childish wonderment!

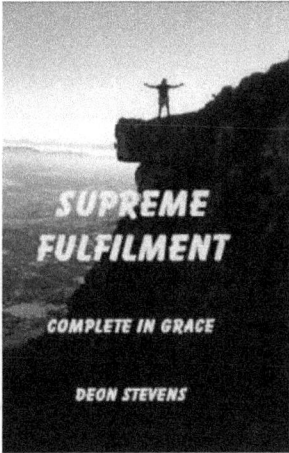

SUPREME FULFILMENT

COMPLETE IN GRACE

DEON STEVENS

Fulfilment in life—the ultimate prize! It is something that one would expect to find in religion. Afterall, religion makes many claims. But these claims are often beyond our reach. That's because they are not obtainable through piety; they are gifts—they are ours by grace! Yet, religion in its wisdom, has seen fit to malign grace, seeing it as permission to sin.

Jesus is not the founder of a religion; He opposes religion! He made His feelings patently clear—He did not appreciate religiosity. He never uttered a single word of accusation to sinful humanity, yet never had a single kind word for religious people.

Oodles of fulfilment can be found in grace! Feelings of inferiority and self-doubt simply cannot survive its empowering edification. It inspires faith and godliness, and makes life enormously fulfilling!

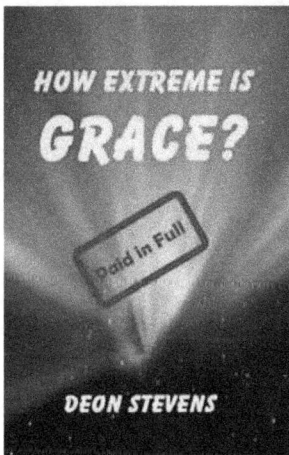

HOW EXTREME IS GRACE?

Paid in Full

DEON STEVENS

Grace, the most treasured gift of all, is under fire from a most unlikely foe—Christendom itself! Grace is often perceived to be at odds with holiness. But it takes more than good intentions to achieve holiness—it takes being loved. Holiness is love in action, and we have no better example of it than in God's grace. Sadly, when Christendom reduces grace, it reduces redemption.

"In Christ", we are so much more than mere mortals. In reality, we have what Christ has! This knowledge opens the door to enormous possibilities. Although the price has been paid in full, we may have to make some mind adjustments before benefiting from the payment.

If we were to discover that religion is holding us back from God's best, would we be prepared to walk away from it?

Love empowering capsules

Take one a Day

Deon Stevens

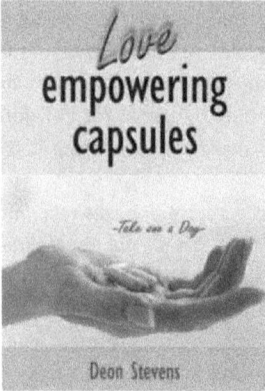

Daily Grace Reading.

Believing in God's grace is one thing—a wonderful thought in theory, but how do we apply it to our daily living?

Where did we get the idea that God is a small-minded bookkeeper, tallying up our failures and successes on a score sheet? How we score in life has no bearing upon our entitlement to God's favour. We are the objects of His furious love pursuit, and we can luxuriate in this liberating knowledge. If Christians are guilty of anything, it would be navel gazing. So much time is spent with self-introspection, self-recrimination and self-condemnation. Somehow we have lost sight of the fact that we are made right because of what Christ did, and not because of what we did. When we discover how highly God esteems us, exactly as we are right now, our self-esteem gets a shot in the arm. Our new sense of worthiness emboldens us to expect more from God. You are not highly favoured because you are holy; you are highly favoured because you are His dearly loved child.

* 9 780620 359313 *